Desire

Bilingual Press/Editorial Bilingüe

General Editor
Gary D. Keller

Managing Editor
Karen S. Van Hooft

Associate Editors
Karen M. Akins
Barbara H. Firoozye

Assistant Editor
Linda St. George Thurston

Editorial Board
Juan Goytisolo
Francisco Jiménez
Eduardo Rivera
Mario Vargas Llosa

Address:
Bilingual Press
Hispanic Research Center
Arizona State University
P.O. Box 872702
Tempe, Arizona 85287-2702
(602) 965-3867

Desire

Alma Luz Villanueva

Bilingual Press/Editorial Bilingüe
TEMPE, ARIZONA

ISBN 0-927534-76-2

Library of Congress Cataloging-in-Publication Data

Villanueva, Alma, 1944–
    Desire / Alma Luz Villanueva.
       p.   cm.
    ISBN 0-927534-76-2 (alk. paper)
    1. Mexican American women—Poetry. I. Title.
PS3572.I354D47 1998
811'.54—dc21   98-11916
                                           CIP

PRINTED IN THE UNITED STATES OF AMERICA

Back cover photo by Leon Canerot
Cover and interior by John Wincek, Aerocraft Charter Art Svc.

Acknowledgments

Excerpt from *Belles Saisons: A Colette Scrapbook* compiled by Robert Phelps. Copyright © 1978 by Robert Phelps. Reprinted by permission of Farrar, Straus & Giroux, Inc., and Random House (UK and Commonwealth).

Excerpt from *Portrait of an Artist: A Biography of Georgia O'Keeffe* reprinted by permission of The Georgia O'Keeffe Foundation (see p. 22).

"The Madonna Diaries" appeared in *Vanity Fair*, 1996 (see p. 111).

Some of these poems originally appeared in the following journals and books: *Prairie Schooner* (1995); *Caprice* (March 1996); *Blood Root* (Place of Herons Press, 1977); *Poems. Third Chicano Literary Prize* (Univ. of California, Irvine, 1977); *After Aztlán: Latino Poets of the Nineties* (David R. Godine, 1992); *A Formal Feeling Comes* (Story Line Press, 1994); *In Other Words: Literature by Latinas of the United States* (Arte Público, 1994); *Unsettling America* (Penguin Books, 1994); *Daughters of the Fifth Sun* (Riverhead Books, 1995); *Paper Dance: 55 Latino Poets* (Persea Books, 1995); *The Best American Poetry 1996* (Scribner's, 1996); *Contemporary Authors Series, Vol. 24* (Gale Research, 1996); *The Language of Literature* (Houghton Mifflin, 1996); *The World's Best Poetry* (Roth Publishing, 1996); *Floricanto Sí! Contemporary U.S. Latina Poetry* (Penguin Books, 1997); and *I've Always Meant to Tell You: Letters to Our Mothers* (Pocket Books, 1997).

Contents

"Everything I want . . . but even that would not be enough."

—Colette (in her eighties, from *Belles Saisons: A Colette Scrapbook,* one of her last books)

HOWLING

THE WOLF AT THE DOOR

1.

The wolf slipped into the supermarket—
someone muttered, "Goddamn dog,
people should take care of their goddamned
dogs." The wolf's paws

scratched the shiny floors, her
nose twitched nervously and the
lights blinded her. There were no
smells, no wind, no sun; there

were people looking hungrily
from side to side. The wolf
climbed up on a shelf and got videoed
by a camera. All she smelled was

boredom and fear. She was no longer
curious, not even a mouse. The wolf
stuck her muzzle up and howled. Then,
she disappeared.

2.

The wolf, upon seeing a collar on
the dog, refused to enter the dog's
house and be fed, so, supposedly,
she starved: you know, I don't

believe this. I mean, maybe she
was shot and skinned and made
into a fur coat: but I know
a wolf can always hunt.

3.

You see the woman with the wild
hair smelling apples just to see
if they're real, the way she squeezes
the hamburger and shakes the milk

around, just to see if they're real.
You see, the woman is a wolf
with the power to open doors.
She scowls at the camera's eye.

4.

She will go home and make tacos,
pick up a photo magazine and read
about a German camp survivor
who supervised 2,000 children

made to carry small stones, who
were fed soup with bits of potatoes
and human flesh. This is when
the woman puts her muzzle skyward

and howls like a wolf. This is when
there's no camera, no witness, and she
is thankful she's part animal, so the
terrible burden of her humanness

will not crush her soul.
This is when she lets
the wolf in: the wolf who
waits at the door.

LONGING (Instinct)

(HER) DESIRE

I dream an old woman at the end
of her life, in her eighties; her hair

is long, beautiful, white; her body
is strong. I bring her tea in a

plain bronze pot, cups; I offer her
food; she refuses food. I cover her

with a quilt and I see it is made
from the night sky, all the galaxies

revolving around it; stars, suns, planets;
all of Creation. Then, I see there are words

on the inner quilt and I realize it is her
life. I say, "Why don't you read all of

it?" She tells me, "No, not yet." I cover
her with Creation. I know she is me,

and on my birth day, this is my gift from the Dream.
Words, my desire. Words, my death.

October 4, 1991

INDIAN SUMMER RITUAL

I was born in Indian Summer,
by the sea, at sun set—

I slid from my mother's womb,
face to the sea—

I felt a dolphin leap
from the sea for joy—

I cried in agony because
I was naked, cold, beached—

It was Indian Summer
and the clouds were purple—

It was Indian Summer
and Venus glowed in the West—

It was Indian Summer
and the moon rose, a ripe, gold melon—

It was Indian Summer
and fire was in the ascendant—

It was Indian Summer
and I danced and danced with dolphins

all the first night of my birth,
until the eagle's cry brought the sun—

It was Indian Summer;
light wolves and dark wolves howled through the day—

It was Indian Summer
and a snake shed its skin.

Then, and only then, was I properly
human.

ANCESTOR

There were times
you and I
were hungry
in the middle of a city of
full bellies
   and we ate bread with
syrup on top, and we joked
and said we ate dessert morning
noon & night, but
we were hungry—
so I took some bottles to the
store and got milk and
stole deviled ham because
it had a picture of the devil
on it and I didn't care—
   my favorite place
      to climb
        and sit was
          Devil's Rock,
            no one else
              would sit there, but
             it was the
               highest place
               around—
taking care
of each other,
an old lady and a child,
being careful
not to need
more than could be given.

   We sometimes went to the
place where the nuns lived and
on certain days they would
give us a bag of food, you
and the old Mexican nun talking,
you were always gracious;
and yet their smell of dead
flowers and the rustle of their robes

always made me feel
shame: I would rather
steal.

And when you held my bleeding nose
for hours, when I'd become
afraid, you'd tell me,
"Todo se pasa."

After you died I learned
to ride my bike to the ocean—
    I remember the night
        we took the 5 Macallister bus
            to the ocean and it was
                storming and frightening,
                    but we bought frozen chocolate
                        bananas on a stick and ate
                            them standing, you and I,
                                in the warm, wet night—
and sometimes I'd wonder why
things had to pass and I'd
have to run as fast as I could
till my breath wouldn't let me
or climb a building scaffold to the
end of its steel
or climb Rocky Mountain and
sit on Devil's Rock
and dare the devil to show his face
or ride my bike till the
end of the streets hit
sand and became ocean,
and I knew
the answer, Mamacita, but
I couldn't even say it to
myself.

Grandmother to mother to
daughter to my daughter,
and to my sons—
the only thing that truly
does not pass is
love—
and you
knew it.

THEY DIDN'T GET ME

They didn't get me.
I feel like the hunted prey that
escaped

> schools
> churches
> office jobs
> city streets
> morals
> anglo culture/western civilization/the democratic process
> dutiful sex free sex no sex
> 9-5
> the perfect mother
> &   "   wife
> IQs/MDs/PHDs/USA
> delivery rooms with drs. in a hurry
> project walls $1/2$ inch thick
> white kids who hate black kids
> black kids who hate white kids
> mexican kids who hate light kids
> people who hate themselves & hate everyone

The city was the hunter
and the streets of my childhood were
peopled with many like me—
> the streets soaked up
oil & blood & rain & tears & dog shit & footsteps &

                                                    love &
children's games & lives & piss & stunted trees & the

                                                    blossoming
trees on Guerrero St. & the hardy weeds that burst

                                                    through
the cracks in spring, especially spring,
and the people, the people, the people.

They told us in school one
time that a beautiful creek
ran down Dolores St., and on

Noe St. Indians fished for their supper, we were told—
    Can't you just see cornfields
spreading all over the Mission?
And all that time,
the earth wasn't confined
to backyards and fences and the 'country'—
    the weeds kept telling
me something I couldn't hear—
the earth was laughing and listening and singing
all that time. All our destruction
can't touch it. It lies in wait.

They can't touch us.
They didn't get us.

Under my flesh/this skin
my heart keeps pumping
    my blood
        laughing and listening and singing inside me
    all on its own
and I'm amazed.

To San Francisco's Mission District,
my childhood ground.

GENIUS

I wanted you to love me, and you did,
for a while, for whatever reasons

you had—but I wanted you to love
me for my heart and soul, my quirky

genius—what makes me dance and sing
for no apparent reason—what makes me

swim past the breakers into the calm—
what makes me laugh till I weep—

what makes me look at beautiful men
and women with longing, appreciation—

what makes me bake brie in garlic, basil,
olive oil, oysters sprinkled with lemon

juice, hot sour French bread, chilled
champagne, yoghurt ice cream, raspberries

on top, a dollop of whipped cream,
more champagne, later sip good brandy—

what makes me start a fire and stare at
it, believing I'm watching the dawn of creation—

what made me love our son more just because
he looked like you as a child, little Indian

boy, our Yaqui—what made me leave
you, your limits, your locks, your heavy

wooden doors that lock out not only
me, but all women—what made me

love you, the small boy, weeping, waiting
for his distant mother—I can't be

your distant mother, I'm the warm, real,
present mother—what makes me love my

children beyond colic, chicken pox, diarrhea,
teenagehood, adulthood, their secret centers

I have touched—what makes me keep on
writing when common sense says, be

a mail carrier or a computer operator—
what keeps me alive.

That. My
desire.

CENTER OF THE SUN

This desire of mine
to stand in the center
of magic; to see

the impossible, to hear
what cannot be heard,
to taste the unspeakable,

to touch the unnamable,
to dream the forbidden,
to love the Universe,

its flawed perfection,
while watching shiny, black
dolphins (who menstruate and

suckle as I do, some of them
carrying young in their ancient
bodies; I feel their desire

as they breathe and dive,
breathe and dive, so perfectly;
their desire to continue forever

and ever and ever this dance
of sea and sun, smooth
silky skin, so sensitive

to touch; when one grazed
me, swimming up the left
side of my body, I remembered

how I am of one skin,
how I am of one desire,
how I am of one Universe,

ever expanding, dying, birthing,
carrying her young in her ancient
body; flawed; perfect; dancing

forever and ever in the center
of magic, in spirals of magic
made by the light of so many

Suns and Seas and Skins and
Desires). I share this temporary
island with two friends; I share

their wonder, this magic, and send
my desire, as usual, to the center
of the Sun (and every Sun before

it; the Universe remembers, carrying
her young in her ancient body, ever
expanding, rippling with rhythms

of orgasms, spirals of orgasms).
My body remembers the body of the
shiny, black dolphin; how we

arch towards the center
of the sun's
desire.

To Carmen and Leon

POWER

You come from a line of
healing women: doctoras, brujas.

Doctors, sorceresses. Though actually,
in the Spanish dictionary, brujo is

sorcerer, conjurer, wizard—while
bruja is witch, hag, owl. HA!

Then owl it shall be. Your great-
grandmother was an owl; your great-

great-grandmother was an owl,
and your mother is a witch,

a hag, and an owl. Witch and hag
has always—in time, only 5,000 years

or so, before that Her magic and
Her beauty shone—meant a woman with

power. Your great-great-grand
mother, Isidra, traveled Sonora

healing, and she married five
times, each time a better man;

your great-grandmother, Jesús, married
to a man of god, healed from wild

weeds and flowers picked from
vacant lots in Los Angeles.

Your grandmother, Lydia, heard
the healing music through her finger

tips, but the music burned her:
witch, hag, witch. And I, your

mother, hear the word, healing
me, you, us, and though I burn,

I fly, too: owl, hawk, raven, my
eagle. Hummingbird, sparrow, jay,

mockingbird, snow owl, barn owl,
great horned owl, pelican, golden

eagle. So, daughter, healer, take my
name: be a witch, a hag, a sorceress.

Take your power and fly like all
the women before you.

Fly Antoinette Therese
Villanueva.

To Antoinette, at thirty,
upon taking her great-grandmother's
name and becoming an R.N.

DELICIOUS DEATH

Memory: You were fifteen in the mountains,
your friends were going hunting,
you wanted to go.

Cold, autumn day—sky of steel
and rifles, the shade of bullets. We
fought. I didn't want to let you go.

And you stood up to me, "My friends are
going, their parents let them hunt, like
am I some kind of wimp or what, Mom . . ."

We walked into Thrifty's to buy the bullets,
you would use one of their rifles—I imagined
you being shot or shooting another eager boy/man.

"What you kill you eat, do you understand?"
I stared each word into your eyes. As you
walked away, I said to the Spirits, "Guard

this human who goes
in search of
lives."

*   *   *

You brought home four small quail.
I took them, saying, "Dinner." I stuffed
them with rice, apples, baked them in garlic,

onions, wine. "Tonight, Mom?" "Yes, tonight."
I plucked the softest tail feathers and as you
showered, I placed them in your pillow case:

"May the hunter and
the prey be
one.

May the hunter truly
be a human
being.

May the hunter eat
and be eaten in
time.

May the boy always
be alive in the
man."

*	*	*

We ate, mostly in silence—
I felt you thinking, I just
killed this, what I'm chewing . . .

On the highest peaks the first
powder shines like the moon—
winter comes so quickly.

On your face, soft, blond hair (yes, this
son is a gringo) shines like manhood—
childhood leaves so quickly.

The wonder of the hunt is on my tongue,
I taste it—wild, tangy, reluctant—
this flesh feeds me well.

I light the candles and thank the quail
in a clear voice—I thank them for their
small bodies, their immense, winged souls.

"God, Mom, you're making me feel like a
killer." "Well, you are, and so am I."
Swallowing, swallowing this delicious death.

To my son, Marc

An Act of Creation

They keep rounding them up
through the centuries, killing
the innocent, so easily—

the babies, the children,
the screaming mothers—
the men who do not beg

for mercy. Yes, yes, they
keep rounding up the victims,
again and again—their only

heirloom/possession: poverty.
When I was a young mother, I
didn't fully realize this—
in my stupidity, I thought

the children were spared.

And when I thought of wolves
and lambs, I thought of
one or the other. A wolf.
A lamb. One bloodthirsty, eating
raw, red meat. One gentle, nibbling

grass. Now, twenty years later, they
still round up the innocent, or
corral them (as in South Africa),
slowly starving their flesh and
spirit to death. The enemy

kills the enemy's children.

A stubborn man fasts for
the farmworkers—their children
are not born whole, and ours
will not be born whole. That

is an act of creation.

Like painting a mural, a
watercolor, like composing
a symphony, like writing
a story, a poem.

That is when the lamb
and the wolf lie down,
together, and make extraordinary,
exquisite, ecstatic. Love.

Until the next round-up.

Or until we learn better—
that without the lamb, the
wolf starves, and without the
wolf, the lamb grows slow
and stupid. Yes, I understand

why the stubborn man
does not eat, pretending
to be a lamb, inviting
the wolves to feast
upon his sweet, brown

flesh. His spirit.

To César Chávez

PULSE

"My center does not come from my mind—" *

1.

I wish to plant sunflowers,
immense faces of the sun,

tilting toward the sun all day,
dreaming in the moonlight, starlight.

Why do I love sunflowers?
Why do I love the sun?

Because they're yellow.
Because the sun is

hot.

*". . . it feels in me like a plot of warm
moist well tilled earth with the sun
shining hot on it—"*

2.

Kayaking out through fog
to sun, baby otters, twenty
to a group, lie on their backs
(seaweed is their bed), turning

toward the sun. We sit, side
by side, eating cherries, ripened
to perfection, facing the sun.
Why?

Because the sun is hot.

---

*The citations that precede each section are from Georgia O'Keeffe in
a letter to author Jean Toomer, in *Portrait of an Artist* by Laurie Lisle.

*". . . I do know that the demands of my plot
of earth are relentless if anything is to grow
in it, worthy of its quality . . ."*

3.

Core of all life—Great Destroyer.
Where you shine, all life begins.

Where you shine, all life perishes.
Yet, we look for you and look for you,

and we would face you, in the Great Darkness.
You, Great Joy, Song, Word, Sight.

You, the Great White Light.

*". . . It seems I would rather feel starkly
empty than let any thing be planted that
can not be tended to the fullest possibility
of its growth . . ."*

4.

To be empty and be filled with the sun.

To be empty and be filled with the moon.

To be empty and be filled with the stars.

To be empty and be filled with the void.

To be empty and be filled with creation:

a song,
a story,
a painting,
a child,
a city,
a garden,
a temple,
knowledge, wisdom, law, love.

To be empty and be filled with darkness.

To be empty and be filled with light.

To be full and give birth to the

impossible.

*". . . If the past year or two or three has
taught me anything it is that my plot of earth
must be tended with absurd care—By myself
first—and if second by someone else it must
be with absolute trust . . ."*

5.

To trust?

To love?

Myself first.

Trust me (it's the only way).

Watch the sunflowers bloom,

spilling seeds into our hands;

a feast for the eyes and tongue.

I bloom in trust.

I trust the color yellow:

desire, fulfilled—

desire, unfulfilled.

O, endless desire:

empty/full   empty/full.

I trust my desire,

endlessly.

". . . It seems it would be very difficult
for me to live if it were wrecked again
just now."

6.

Worlds without
end, sun
on my
earth.

Toward summer, June 1991

THE LOVER

What is the difference
between sexuality and sensuality,

we discuss   oh so
calmly . . . I spin

on the words
sexuality   sensuality

as though they were
worlds, civilizations

I've been studying:
"Sexuality is localized in

the genitals," I say . . .
"an energy that keeps

us hungry, hunting,
stalking. Sexuality seizes,

tames, conquers, gloats
and howls with victory,

and we are all proof of this
momentary victory, the trophy."

I pause
and continue:

"Sensuality. Rose petals, thick
grass, deep water, fragrant neck,

newborn-in-the-arms, suckling
milk and light, lover's lips, tender

tongues, frying onions, luscious
sauce simmering, to be poured over

meat slid from bone,
done, perfect, surrendered,

cooked, for, your, pleasure,
the perpetual sound of the sea,

aching, longing, roaring, singing,
singing, roaring, longing, aching,

the never ever ever ending
delight, no trophies,

delight, no proof;
I give my children back

to their lives, their senses,
their most private and secret

dreams, where we conquer worlds
and then wisely relinquish them

in order to praise the Lover
(delight),

worlds without ever
ending," I murmur

as I watch summer disrobing
and   oh   so   slowly

enter the irresistible coolness
on the 26th of June.

(Renewing the)
VOW

Dawn. Fog. Thin and mysterious
over the still, untouched lake.
I am alone with the lake
and I am happy to be alone
with eternity. Silence fills
me, death kisses my lips.
What a bride I am, pregnant
with eternity, wanting nothing
more than this perfect
solitude, the sun rising
at my back. I hear it hissing
like a snake. I feel it bite
me with its warmth. "Yes,"
I whisper, "I am
willing."

Sierra Madres in August—

THE WIND

I wanted to be your friend
    (the mountains roared like
      Vietnam, you said)—

I wanted to be your lover
    (the lightning kept me up
      with wonder, staring)—

I wanted to accept the light
    (the rain was soft and chill,
      I made us tea, laughing)—

I cannot translate the language of
the mountains, or give you light,
or take your darkness, or ease
your memories, or make you wonder—

I can only want.
The rest is up
to you. My wanting
is the wind—invisible

and real. It clings
to nothing, changes everything
in its path in some small way.
I want the wind.

The Sierras in August—

SWEET STRANGER

The father's sperm, gift from

a stranger—

my life, a life among

strangers—

when I stand to read my poems

or teach a class full of

strangers—

I see myself in every face,

yet unique, distinct—

the gift of life,

from me to you,

sweet stranger.

         ⋆   ⋆   ⋆

Each flower unique—
each stone,
each shell,
each footprint

in the gold-flecked sand—
nothing is familiar—
everything is newly born—
the Earth has changed from yesterday—

the air,
the sun,
shadows,
our fingernails are longer—

our cells explode into newness—
only newness will kill us, this effort
to be reborn, again, into the sweet,

sweet stranger.

EMPTY CIRCLE

This light reminds me of my death—
this light of freshness after a brief
rain edged in storm clouds,
butterflies dancing, touching wings—

the ripe roses wet with light,

they open, slowly, to their deaths,

so beautifully, so beautifully—

they know their time will come again.

Already their future selves nestle
in the root; the old thorns prepare
themselves for birth. Nothing stays
the same. Not even our death.

I will die in the afternoon, sunset,
into the freshness of a storm, the
night an onyx ring—I will be the
emptiness in the circle and death

will wear me like an ornament—I will
be a shadow on death's finger, a slender
nothingness. All I ask for in this
life is the sun.

That's all. I want.

SINGING (Hunger)

SHAMELESS

Bless the owl and the eagle,
the chicken and the hawk—
I dreamt I was about to fly
standing on the rim of a cliff—

I asked my wings to grow,
my eagle wings—instead,
Wisdom told me to go to a bowl
full of chicken feathers, to coat

myself and fly. I began to laugh
until I cried, and, laughing, I flew
over endless beauty,
over endless time.

Wisdom laughs in the face
of eagle feathers, chicken
feathers; Wisdom only
wants to fly.

Dream, January 1993

WARRIOR IN THE SAND

I want to be a black belt in
Kung Fu at fifty—

I want to fall in love at fifty,
sixty, seventy, eighty—

I want to wear my bikini (or be
naked) until I die—

I want to dance and sweat at
my pre-death party,

and get drunk on champagne
with my exuberant guests—

and when I've achieved transformation,
I want no crying.

I want laughter. I want someone
to recite my poetry in a loud,
clear voice. I want babies and
children to be in the room, and

I want the poems to mean nothing
to them. I want to peek through
their eyes, once, before my long,
dangerous journey home. Home

to the spiral that burns with
its terrible pulsing love.
And let the children laugh with
that recognition before they forget.

It's so easy to forget—
making love, cooking food,
finding shelter, giving birth,
fighting pain, seeking joy.

Will my own children be there—
grandparents by that time—

will I look through my
great-great grandchildren's

eyes—who knows. I've
insisted they take their freedom
so that I may have mine. Freedom
demands nothing, and love

gives everything. I have
wandered between these
extremes—mountain to ocean,
silence to shout, poet to

woman, counting the stones,
the shells, the feathers in
my pockets, fingering my solitude
as a child runs ahead, singing.

At the edge of the tide, in the
twilight, is a human figure
with arms and legs, a body, a
head, with no particular gender—

a woman/man. Spirals edge its
body, and a spiral is drawn down
the center, where the throat, heart,
lungs and genitals should be.

Feathers grow from its head.
I laugh with recognition and,
kneeling, plant mine. I place
a perfect, white shell in its

dream-eye. Now, I see, I was
saving everything for the warrior
in the sand, who will be washed
away by morning.

Santa Cruz, California

THE HEART MUST BE BROKEN
AGAIN AND AGAIN, OR
IT GROWS HARD

I'm in a Washington DC hotel
in the middle of the night—
I waken in tears, dreaming

my sun-haired son around two,
his little body, how I loved
it, the meteor streak of his

movements, the flash of lightning,
his smile, mischief, his eyes
so terribly alive, his insistence

to be born won my heart: I waken
when I realize, in the dream, he
is grown, a man; why, I ask, does

this break my heart?
Is it that when a force so vital
enters this world (mine is similar)

you cannot bear to see it dimmed—
is that why I spit and fight, refusing
to let the lightning leave my eyes,

preferring to be terribly alive—
was that your message, Marc,
your child to mine?

On a business trip—

THE GIFT OF BREATH

My son, almost a teenager,
feels my sadness in the deepening
twilight—the sun at the edge

of the world, going to the other edge—
a fragile star in the west, just
beginning to speak to the translucent

crescent—I've just cooked a tasty
dinner, the wine was white and full
and good—oh, I'm sad, just about

human things (you know—the ego,
the superego, the id, the self . . .
i.e., joy, sorrow, rage, ecstasy)—

well, my almost-grown son goes
out to the twilight, barefoot,
without a jacket, in the chill,

to blow bubbles in the darkening air.
I bring him a jacket and watch the bubbles
float—he blows a string of them, eight in a row,

small ones (they're funny, the way they
squabble and dance for space, then float,
and float away, into the darkness, perhaps

trying to catch the sun or greet
the moon or speak to the star, now
singing). He patiently blows a large

one, an immense one, a miracle
of sorts—rainbow-hued in the
center, shimmering with itself,

and a glow of red surrounds it;
he blows another large one and it,
too, is a miracle of shape and color

(these bubbles do not squabble or dance;
they simply hold to the darkness, filled with
my son's breath, his love for me).

I accept these simple
miracles, even as they
pop.

To El Jules

CHANCE

Yes, I've told you,
"You are a royal fucking pain in the ass,"

and you are my mother. I do not
forgive you for leaving me at

the Emporium in downtown San Francisco
when I was five. I do not

forgive you for betraying
my seven-year-old trust when we lay

in bed talking after I caught
my molester: "It's your fault he's going

to jail, you know." The years when
you neglected my existence or tortured

me to rage (the time I broke the
window with my hand, the tiny scar

on my right-hand baby finger still
hurts if it's bumped just so). Or when

you shook my daughter's crib violently
as she cried for her mother at seven days

old, and I slept through it at fifteen;
I woke and saw you screaming, "Shut up!

Shut up!" I leapt to my feet,
grabbed you, threw you against

the wall and yelled, "If you ever
touch my baby again, I'll kill

you!" And then you tried to give
her away—I escaped

with a friend to a flea-trap
over a bar with loud music;

she and I (15 and 16), and my daughter,
slept in the same bed. The time

you left me with a ten-year-old
friend and her mother, who didn't have

much to eat, and you didn't return
for days, and they took me to

the place where unloved children
are taken to be among strangers

(and, as when you left me at five,
I took care of myself and called

your sister, the one who lives in
a trance, while you dance,

while you dance. I have done
both: the trance of the unloved:

the dance of the unloved).
I could go on and on and on—

the time you refused me food,
"I fucked him for this food!"

I could go on and on and on—
but I won't. Well, what is

it? I ask myself. What is it
about this woman that moves

me? (At 78 you refuse self-pity
as you walk through the mall

making friends with all the sales
people—they know you by name;

you rise for work at 4 am to shower,
apply your make-up, dress in bright

colors that tend to clash; your retirement
party from full-time work will be

celebrated on the Cinco de Mayo, Mexican
Independence Day, birth place of your

mother and father, your people—you,
in your beautiful, light skin, who

always avoided the sun, your blonde
wig—at 78 you don't look your age—

privately, you tell me, "It's my
Indian blood, the Yaqui de mi

Mamá.") A story, a memory stored
in my body, in my childhood cells;

when I was three you refused
to let my father's racist family keep

me; when you carried me on a hot Louisiana
dirt road; when your mother's voice rang

true in your mind: "Bring the child home
to her people." And you did.

And so, at the very beginning of my life, then,
and the end of yours, now,

I'll take this chance (no trance,
no dance) and say I love

you, knowing full well who you are,
and who I am.

TRUST

I wouldn't be surprised if I opened
the front door and nuclear winds
were blowing, the sky a crazy color,

like a tornado, everything swept away—
my child, myself, and everyone else
(this is only a fantasy, now) (I know

the power of words, I know)—the sun
strolling down the street, tired of her
place, a distant star—she wants to embrace

us, make us disappear—well, okay, what
does this mean?

Who do you trust when love turns its
back on you? When the ozone tatters,

bit by bit? When wars are more popular than
teaching children? When people have no memory

of what a bed was like, clean sheets? When
children, everywhere, go to sleep hungry? When

the children of Baghdad are slaughtered?
When South Africa comes to its senses?

When the rainforests curse the sky?
When all the murdered in Latin America

return to their families, intact and singing?
When the radiation at Chernobyl stops killing

the innocent? When children in our cities
stop dying for lack of hope, stray bullets,

the crack dealer's promises, our leader's
promises, their convenient lies

to the children of the poor, the forgotten?
When our Drug Wars turn into Fierce Peace:

medical coverage, dental coverage, food, clothing,
shelter, real, substantial, *free* education? When

the birds become mute and tired of flying? When
Spring turns her back on us, withholding her

matrix, source; whispering in the wind,

"There was a web, but you destroyed it—

there was a seed, but you crushed it—

there was a way, but you forgot."

Oh, and me standing in the sun, praising her
to the very end.

TAKES TWO TO TANGO

I went out and bought a
lovebird, yes, a
lovebird. I feel

like a man who goes to a
whore, a lovely, colorful whore,
and buys her love.

Now I feed her, saying her
name over and over: Mango, Mango.
Mango, where's your tango?

ONLY LOVE MAY ENTER

1.
Desperate for love,
I went out and bought
a lovebird; I have

visions of letting her fly
around the house, at large,
and tacking a sign on the door

saying, "Beware of lovebird."
            or
        "Mango, where's your tango?"
            or
        "Lovebirds flying free."
            or
                        "Only love may enter."

2.
Now, I'm not so desperate.
I've said nice things to my self.
I lit the candle and sang the song.

I've touched the wound of others
and found it full of bright
blood like my own.

I've touched my own wound
and found it raw and sensitive,
singing to the world,
                    Only love may enter.

3.

And when you enter, the room is bathed
in light. Leave your childhood behind,
but not your child.

Be prepared to love; what's life
but a long/short preparation
for the room of your dying,

when it fills with light.
When only love may enter.
Love me now, love.

（The Mango Poems, #3）

MEDUSA AND I

1.
Tenderness is so long in coming;
can you treat it as money to be
spent? An investment? A natural

resource to be plundered? Or what?
I ask you, Mango, chirp twice
if you think tenderness should be ex

changed on the common market—
chirp once if you think not—
you stare at me with your

innocent/knowing lovebird eyes
like Buddha holding the flower up
to the gathering, like Isis suckling

Horus, like Medusa and her sexy
snakes waiting for the man brave
enough to fuck her, discovering

he could die of tenderness, this fucking
not turning him to stone, but turning
him into a loving man, her stare, centuries

of stored tenderness, her snakes dance
and writhe round her head, FUCK ME, the
awe-ful ecstasy, you will remember, the

flesh and blood, fuck me, you will re
member, O brave, man, truly brave, man,
t e n d e r n e sssssssssssssssssssssssssss

2.
The other night I went dancing alone—
I left my lovebird in her cage
with food and water, jungle dreams.

Medusa came and sat next to me,
stretching her legs for the music—
her snakes slept round her head,

contentedly—that morning she'd sold
her tenderness on the common market.
She said, "A prostitute compassionate

am I"—her snakes lifted their heads
up to see who she was talking to, they
flicked their tongues. Medusa and I

shared some grass, talked of our children
and danced. She danced like a virgin,
her head thrown back, her arms raised,

inviting no man—but I danced
to every man in the room, and then, again,
to no man. I love the company of whores.

"A prostitute compassionate am I." Who
can sell it? Who can give it away?
Only a whore. Only a virgin.

3.
O Mango, when Medusa started talking
shop—like how the price of a head job
has gone up due to AIDS, and she

added, "Men like to give, you know,"
then she smiled—she melted my heart.
And when I said, " When we're not intimate

I don't want to fuck him," she said,
"You could send him to me"—I laughed.
Then we passed her pipe again and shared

a bottle of Chablis. Last night as my
lover fucked me, I imagined he was a paying
customer, he imagined he was a brave man—

and as my knees went up to his chest,
as he kneeled, he found the tip of my
tenderness as I moaned, head thrown back,

hands pulling him closer—I fucked every man,
I fucked only him, I fucked no man,
and all my snakes

4.
danced. And all my snakes danced.
Mango, centuries of stored tenderness
can make you cry.

SOME KIND OF FREEDOM

1.

Mango, I wear a Japanese kimono,
but it reminds me of China—
all the Asian people walking
down the mountain of my body.

Lines of them, and they all look
like farmers, workers, just people.
I wonder where they're coming
from: work, the fields, a failed

revolution. . . . In China, in June,
when the plum blossoms quiver
and begin to fall, dreaming
of their fat, yellow fruit,

thousands of people were shot (I
read of a three-year-old child who
was killed by smashing her skull—
the plums, the plums, the fragile, white

     blossoms)
               fighting for some
kind of freedom. Here, in our country,
we watched by television; they showed

only the grown-ups shouting,
bleeding, dying;
and that was bad
enough.

2.

Mango, I bought four cakes
of rose soap;
the golden sticker,
the flower and bee—

usually, it gives me much
pleasure to look at them
unopened. I ask myself:
should I have bought

these rose soaps from
China? Should I wash
my body with their sweet
scent? Should I stand

in the shade so the same
sun we share won't warm
me? The moon? The stars?
Should all three-year-olds

stop talking to grown-ups?
Should I burn my kimono?
Will the workers and farmers,
the people, be safe if I do?

3.
Mango, in a lifetime, centuries
ago, I was a Chinese woman,
a writer—I preferred silk
and little luxuries. I had

no children. It was then,
that life, when I acquired
an exquisite taste for
beauty, and my love

for the perfect
word. It was then
that I thought the whole
world was China.

Now, I'm here, looking
there, thinking of the one
who wears us on her body,
her mountain, in beauty.

To China, June 1989—
From the T'ang Dynasty
and Shing Moo

(The Mango Poems, #5)

"Having no answers to
questions will not make
them go away."
—*From a fortune cookie*

UROBOROS

(The circular snake biting Its
tail is the symbol of the psychic state
of the beginning, of the original situation . . .)
—Erich Neumann, *The Great Mother*

Mango,
I'm back. I went into the mountains,
first with a friend, a fellow-teacher—
first to Silver Lake bearing brandy,
tequila—we made a fire that laughed
with its heat, a fire that thought her
self beautiful simply because
she was hot, untouchable, so very

necessary. At Silver we told each
other stories that made us laugh until
we cried: our defeats and victories
(brandy to tequila to brandy to tequila).
We sat on stone and praised the purity
of Gaia, Lake, Stone, Moon, Stars, The
Silence (the way it was, the way it
was, in the beginning). The moon rose,

a waxing crescent (the way it is,
the way it is, in the end). We re
membered lovers, children, friends,
husbands, the dead, enemies,
desires, defeats: we laughed (brandy
to tequila to brandy to tequila). We
slid like girls into sleeping bags, crystals
and knives close by—a doe's eyes shone

like rubies in the flash light, twin fires,
but she did not laugh, staring
silently at me I turned off the
light and let her go. Towards dawn
an owl, a she-owl, called her death,
her prey, the sun to her; the burning
star we require to live. There was no
sadness in her song (as it is now, as it is *now*).

(Did we defeat defeat?)

Next, we walked the path and climbed the stones,
touching trees, speaking to the Mother Tree,
to the Father Tree, to the Entrance, the
Gateway to the Goddess; she accepts
our spirits going in and lets us go as
we leave Gold, the lake of Gold. Sun
and water blind us into silence, and in
that silence our wombs speak. We praise

our friendship, we praise other women's
victories, those that heal, continually, the
rape of their childhood bodies, minds, spirits;
those who seek refuge in ten, twenty, thirty,
forty selves in one body, one mind, one spirit,
the pain so immense it must be shared. We
share their pain, we share their stories; we
share this knowledge with She Who Knows (everything).

(Did we defeat loneliness?)

I speak of my desires. You speak of your
desires. I speak of love. You speak of love.
What we want. What we need. We speak
singularly. We speak together. I scream my
eagle's cry, looking for her. You scream your
low owl's cry (the Goddess-Lake-Goddess eats
your voice—all winter you will sing in ice, in
spring you will join the Many Voices—in

the summer your own voice will call
you back). You lost a treasured earring,
the required omen, and as we drive away,
down the road to your leaving, a huge
shadow touches us: the she-eagle flies,
her shadow. Her touch is dark and chilling;
I know what she wants. Yes, I say,
I promise I'll return in four days.

(Did we defeat lies?)

I return, alone, to Silver and Gold,
carrying one lovely bottle of wine. The
wind and silence sculpt me, as well as
sweat, the honest strength of my body.
The Goddess draws me into her in silence;
I swim in silence; I eat in silence.
Wings, broad, silent wings turn my head
and she swoops in widening circles of air,

over the rim of granite, then she screams,
my eagle. I know this lake, this granite,
this shore will outlive (pray it will, pray)
me. I know my fear is tempered by my courage
(pray it is, pray). I know that I live to
love, I live to love (praise the Goddess,
praise). I know the sting of talons upon my
neck and I obey. I accept your awe-ful gift.

(Did love defeat me?)

Six pure white birds gave me an answer:
three made a pyramid to the left—
three made a pyramid to the right—
then, together, they spelled h o L
The whole   holy   Energy to me.
Energy through me. The answer:
        △ h o L △

You know the song,
Flyforeverintolove,
where defeat asks the questions
and answers them too.

Flyforeverintolove
where the answers know
the questions, waiting for
the gift of your song/fear/courage

(Did courage defeat me?)

A twenty-seven-year-old woman was burned
to death, bombed in Beirut; were her children
with her, I wonder. They arrest a group
of people in Colombia; they torture the men,
rape the women, scatter the children to the
wind. In South Africa to be Black is a
crime punishable by poverty, torture, death.
In China it's a crime to dream of freedom.

Why do our leaders dream of nothingness?
Why is the male God so terribly lonely?
Why is fear danced into violence?
Why are women feared?
Why is the Earth round?
Why is the Goddess singing?
Why are we here? Why do we forget?
Why do I need to not know and wonder?

(Did wonder defeat me?)

Here, by the sea, I watch a group
of seagulls devour a fledgling;
they peck its body, its head, and
it's terrible, though I know what
dies, the body, must be eaten, trans
formed. I'm tempted to take it from them,
but I know that they must eat, as I must
eat. The beautiful, foam-blue waves

finally sweep the fledgling, gone.
Aren't the seagulls sleek? Doesn't the
beautiful sea cradle life and death? Isn't
the sun warm? Isn't the wind alive?
Isn't the sunlight on the water, the child's
wet shoulder, beautiful? Isn't the song
of the Goddess singing to the lonely God
beautiful? Why is there no end to beauty?

(Did beauty defeat me?)

My grandchildren call me Mamacita.
My lover calls me Hot Thing.
My friends call me Loyal, Bitch.
My enemies call me Worse.
My poems call me Hey You.
My power calls me Eagle Woman,
    Snake Woman, Wolf Woman,
        Daughter.

When I weep, I end up laughing.
When I laugh, I end up weeping.
When I love, I love too much.
When I hate, I hate too much.
When I ask a question, my
    answer asks a question. In
this way I am never, ever bored;
a snake eating Its own tail.

In my sorrow is a joy.
In my joy is a sorrow.
In my orgasm there is a dying.
In my death there is the ultimate
    p l e a s u r e (It
will always be, it will always be
so). May I teach myself pleasure; others
will teach me pain. Death, teach me love.

So, Mango, I'm willing to die for It.
I'm willing to live for It.
I'm willing to obey Its commands,
and to command It. I'm willing to.

I'm willing. By this name or another,
I will return, in this form or another,
changing names, faces, times. My real
name is Pleasure (it will always be).

(Did I defeat death?)

(Did death defeat me?)

> When I ask a question, my
> answer asks a question. In
> this way I am never, ever, bored;
> a snake eating Its own tail.

> You know the song,
> Flyforeverintolove,
> the gift of your own fear/courage.
> (Hey You, that's enough. . . .)

> △ h o L △

What do you say,
Mango?   (Hey You?)
(Yes?)
       (Hey You?)
                     (Yes?)
     Fly   forever
                  into   love
(Your Lover, Death—The Hottest Thing)

DON'T   FORGET — THESE   ARE

BIRDS,   NOT   LETTERS—

(Hey You?)

       (Yes?)

A snake eating Its own tail.

I'm back,
Mango.

*For Leslie Simon, and
also for Little Wolf*

THINGS OF OUR CHILDHOOD

I watch you defy your death,
climbing the sheer mountain cliff
until you become a dot.
I do not say, "Come back,
you'll kill yourself!" No, I stopped
that a while ago, and I watch you
climb with joy, as I climb with joy;

so I understand, only you go straight up
and I go sideways, then up—but I get
there. We talk and the lake listens,
then the fire, and finally, just the

stars. The first night we sat on granite
as galaxies appeared in the dark, cold
lake; I told you things of my childhood,
and, later, things of your childhood.
I lead, you lead. Mother, son.
Man and woman. Backpacking out,

you go ahead; I stop often, touching
trees, stones, whispering my goodbyes,
knowing there are no goodbyes. Knowing
you will greet me. Soon.

To Marc, in his twenty-first year

DEATH-INTO-LIFE-DREAMING

My daughter and I walk
the early morning beach,
virginal from its dreams
of salt, foam, slap

of cold, Womb of All Life.
"A skull," she points. "Is
it human?" I ask. We turn
it over. "Animal, not

round enough," she says
(a nurse, acquainted with
such things). "Good,"
I say. We leave it to

rest, so white, a shell
gazing up from the sand.
I pick white feathers as
we walk and talk, for

no particular reason: a dark
stone with a copper circle
surrounding it: a smooth,
translucent purple shell.

We return to the beginning:
"I wonder why we didn't see it?"
she asks. "This is why I was saving
these, I guess," I say, going to my

knees, placing all the soft white feathers
on the monster's dream-eye, the dark
stone, purple shell on top, in front
of the soft white feathers. She places

a perfect sand dollar
on the forehead: a skull
made from human hands
(seaweed, ash, feathers, sticks).

Skull to skull: Death to death.
Death, our own sweet monster:
dream us (my daughter and I) as clearly
as possible, that we may deserve

our skulls, empty from your fullness.
Bring the gifts you hoard
for those who honor
the monster, Death-Into-Life-Dreaming.

Autumn Equinox, 1992, Santa Cruz—
To my daughter,
Antoinette

THE WILD MOTHERS MOURN

Oh, child, if you had been
my daughter, oh my child,

my sweet, strong child-woman
at twelve, the edge of your

dancing body, full to its
silver brim with innocence,

its longing to know the mysteries—
you, sweet daughter,

you were stolen,
you were violated,

your dancing body stilled—
but your soul escaped,

singing like a joyous bird
at sunset/sunrise—

you spread your soul-wings,
you sang your soul-song,

you perched on a limb of light,
filling with gold, filling with gold

(the Source, the Unnamable,
to the very brim of knowing).

Take your Time (O, Mother
    of Mysteries), return in

your perfect innocence
    (now you know there

is no death).

       ★   ★   ★

In Cotati, not far from
your parent's house, a wild

woman has come to rest;
she cannot speak or hear,

or even sign to understand,
but she is sweet, they say,

and smiles with understanding,
in her silence, singing, singing

without a word.

      ★   ★   ★

The wild mothers prepare
a place for you to rest

or to return, child.

To Polly Klaas

WILD, WILD CHILD

On my birth day, I'm given
a drawing of the last child I might've

had; she sits in the wilderness,
the forest all around her, wild

animals left to right, and wild
geese fly over her head; she's covered

by a blanket of stars, real ones,
an immense star-butterfly on her lap;

she's transforming into something unknown,
and she smiles without fear, filled

with wonder, curiosity. Instead of
having this child, this daughter

(who I've dreamt more than once, but
she had sea-green eyes), I've

become her. We transform, endlessly,
together. I am her wild, wild mother.

She tells me: "I have never, ever,
ceased to exist. I am your unborn

daughter." We spin   spin   spin   spin
on this perfect planet, she and I,

laughing.

MESTIZA

I'm a Mestiza, a mixed-blood:
Yaqui, Spanish, German, English—
my people from the four corners
of the Earth—

I've been called spic, wetback,
greaser, dirty Indian, bitch, cunt,
ball-buster, dyke, and even gringa.
I've been told, "You're too feminine."

I've been told, "You're too masculine."
I've been told, "God, you're beautiful."
I've been told, "Fuck, you're ugly."
"You're so loving, what, are you trying to

kill me, I love your poetry, all you
do is nag nag nag, you've shown me
the way of my soul, you need medication,
I love your pussy, you're not my mother,

you're a genius, you're a fool,
you're so wise, you're self-centered me me me"—
Yes, I'm a Mestiza, a mixed-blood
human being, glad to be a woman,

I said glad to be a woman, perched
at the edge of the dwindling century,
facing The New, dreaming The Old.
My people are from the four

corners of the Earth—
we are all human,
we are all human—
bleeding, healing. Sometimes loving.

SONG（Food）

JEWELS

I'm swarmed by bees—
10, 20, 30, 40—hundreds.

I kill a few and they sting
me—I begin to panic

until I hear my inner
voice: "Be still, be calm,

be still." Slowly, I center
myself into peace, and the

angry bees begin to land
on my body, crawl with

curiosity (I must keep still),
nestle in my flesh, tired

and trusting. As I gaze at
the sleeping bees, I see

they are tiny, perfect jewels—
they glitter, their tired wings

filtering sunlight, making my body
beautiful.

Dream, January 1994

TWINS: DEATH AND DESIRE

Bob, the first night, you came to my
poetry reading—I saw you
in the audience, your shy/ironic,
expect-nothing-from-the-world

face (the child still alive in the man).
The first poet to read was drunk;
a good poet, but a little crazy,
and some other drunks in the audience

began to taunt him (and this was
an art gallery in San Francisco's North
Beach, usually very pristine): then,
my turn and they started in on me.

I stopped, looked them right in their
unfocused eyes, and said, "I would
appreciate it, very much, if you'd all
shut up, right now." The audience:

"Yeah, why don't you shut up, man!"
"Yeah, shut the fuck up!"
"If you don't like it, leave!"
"Didn't you morons know it was a poetry reading?"

After my reading, applause, compliments
from the audience—then, suddenly,
an explosion from the hall. We all
run out, one of the drunks is thrown

to the floor, two men are kicking him
repeatedly, saying, "You should watch
your mouth, buddy, you fuckingasshole . . ."
And you, Bob, you couldn't stand

it—in a split second, you raised
both arms like an outraged bear,
you growled deep in your throat,
and pushed through the crowd (you

were tall and thin, but wiry, I suppose),
grabbing both men off of their bleeding
victim, saying, "Leave him alone,
goddammit, it's just not fair,

leave him the fuck alone!" And
they did. The man was bleeding from
the eye and cheek, his ribs were
sore. You took control, "Stay back,

I'm a fuckin doctor, just stay back!"
You took the drunk on your motorcycle
to your clinic and patched him up, and
when you returned to the bar where

the poets and audience gathered, I said,
"Well, the idiot had it coming, but
you did the right thing, Bob." "I just
can't stand it, I just can't stand

seeing shit like that." I think of you
today after a skirmish over a car repair
bill (and I won—two men against me)—and
I think of you, Bob, and miss your irrational

warrior's spirit and all that you desired
in spite of your defiant child and all that
you gave, knowing the taste of defeat
from the beginning, but you used it

like salt to flavor your victories.
You are with me, like an ancestor, and
you may share my desire for everything,
and the satisfaction I intend to receive

(and demand for others), because
I am defiant, like you were,
with equal doses of
DESIRE (old friend, old warrior,

old, because now you are dead from
a madman's gun—let's go to the limit—
there's only death and desire—
those ancient, wise, childish

twins).

To Bob Ross, M.D.

CRAZY COURAGE

Why do I think of Michael . . .
He came to my fiction class
as a man (dressed in men's
   clothes); then he came

to my poetry class
as a woman (dressed in women's
   clothes; but he was still
a man under the clothes).

Was I moved in the face of
such courage (man/woman
   woman/man) . . .
Was I moved by the gentleness

of his masculinity; the strength
of his femininity . . .
His presence at the class poetry
reading, dressed in a miniskirt,

high boots, bright purple tights,
a scooped-neck blouse, carrying
a single, living, red rose, in a
vase, to the podium (the visitors,

   not from the class, shocked—
the young, seen-it-all MTV crowd—
into silence as he's introduced,
"Michael . . .") And what it was, I think,

was his perfect dignity, the offering
of his living, red rose to the perceptive,
to the blind, to the amused, to the impressed,
to those who would kill him, and

to those who would love him.
And of course I remember the surprise
of his foamy breasts as we hugged
goodbye, his face blossomed

open, set apart, the pain of it,
the joy of it (the crazy courage
to be whole, as a rose is
whole, as a child is

whole before they're
punished for including
everything in their
innocence).

To Michael B.

WITNESS

I grow weary with blame.
It crowds me—to blame
or be blamed.

It crowds the winter sun,
the waning moon, letting go of
its light, without blame.

It must die, become dark.
The sun is furthest from
the Earth. Do the birds shiver

and blame the sun for being
so far away? Do the otters curse
the sea? Do the whales, the seals?

Does the great snowy owl, swooping
over dazzling fields of snow-light?
Do the butterflies, clinging together,

clustering into one single being, dreaming
the sun's return, the slow movement
of planets; the stars expending their

energies, their white-hot joys, do
they blame the universe because
they will fall, they will fall?

It seems the soul must suffer to awaken
to its hunger—we must bear witness
to the evil, to the good,

which makes the blinding light be born
from the soul—the whitest light,
the harshest light, the clearest light—

the light born from the soul's fire,
the soul's ravenous hunger.
I was born poor and hungry and lost

my safety at ten (an old woman's
love). I was pregnant at fourteen,
sixteen. I was uneducated.

I should be dead. I should be a junkie.
I should be a prostitute. I should be stupid.
Who would I blame?

*   *   *

(Historically, through the ages, or
lifetime after lifetime—I am Spanish,
the Conqueror, the Inquisition, killer

of the innocent, children of the Goddess—
I am English, hungry for empires,
ruthless collector of cultures, mannered

and uncivilized—I am German,
the evil of our century, the messenger
of our time, "Death is relative"—I am

Yaqui Indian, undefeated, proud, magical,
civilized, keeper of the dream—united, in
a rainbow am I, Sudden Rainbow am I.

We are all witness to our human history.
Look, deeply, into your eyes. Look, deeply,
into your heart, my enemy, my love.

We return from the light to span
the darkness with rainbows.
We are the witness.

We are the dreamer.
We are the dreamed.
We are the hungry.)

$\star$　　　$\star$　　　$\star$

So, take our human stories, tell them,
yes, always tell them—cry, laugh, rage.
Then praise. Then rage. Then praise.

again and again and again
Listen to the soul's courageous singing,
fiery light—how she wants to give us

everything: joy, sorrow, rage, praise.
Can we blame
her?

(THE FUTURE)

Day #1

I swim out into the sea, surrounded
by seaweed—a young, dark seal
greets me, his eyes see the future—
two dark pools, two dark mirrors.

His eyes are gentle, not sad;
knowing, not lost; serene, not afraid;
his eyes are at home in his world.
I drape a long piece of seaweed

around my body and float in the sun—
wind speaks to my ears: "Welcome, welcome,
naked human—your gills gone, your fins gone,
your sharp, ripping teeth gone—you are the

future, you and your kind—you, the poet,
whale of the sea, sing to us your
human song. The wise, young seal
has seen your soul."

Day #2

I went shopping for lipstick with my son;
        (dreaming of the ocean,
        swimming in the ocean,
        seaweed round my hips,
        tasting salty foam. . . .)

I chose *Wine with Everything,* and when
the saleswoman repeated it, my son,
startled, asked, "Did she say 'You want everything?' "
like I was being deeply insulted and I might
reach over the counter and pop her in the eye.

I laughed, "Sure, I want everything,
        (the young seal's eyes find me,
        his body as dark as midnight
        in the noonday sun—he knows
        I'm a child, though my soul is old. . . .)

but I guess I'll have to settle for—" I show
him the lipstick. He laughs. . . . my son
is a child, but his soul is old. I see
the past, present, future in his face:
I've always wanted everything (singing. . . .)

Day #3

My hands, in the twilight, one lit candle,
my hands are amazing, two bony miracles;

held the newborn, held the pen,
slapped in anger, caressed in pleasure;

washed the diapers, played with seaweed,
my hands remember what to do so well;

planted the pine, killed the ants,
fed the hummingbirds, caught the kittens;

O, my hands, little workers, little
pleasure seekers, how you love the sea;

how the seal loves you because
you cup the sea, spiral seaweed;

O, my hands, how you reach for the necessary;
O, my hands, how you reach for the miracle.

Day #4

I stand to see the setting full moon—

I touch the morning—

A raven, messenger of the moon, caws—

"The future is here, now, hold it."

The poet of the sky has sung to me—

I sing to her, "Yes, I am here. Now. Here."

I touch the morning—

The sun, the sun.

PEACE #1

Mango, I've entered the age of miracles
    (doesn't the hummingbird eat my sugar?)—

A seal slid across my leg
    (wasn't I terrified?)—

Four dolphins danced for my pleasure
    (wasn't I awed?)—

Kayaking into the fog, pelicans gliding
    (wasn't I smiling?)—

My body hums sex, hunger, truth, feast
    (am I not grateful?)—

My spirit willingly lives in my body, singing
    (am I not listening?)—

My words are my own, yet given
    (am I not speaking?)—

Mango, I've entered the age of miracles
    (doesn't the eagle greet me?)—

Yes,
oh yes,
I've entered the miracle,
trembling. Singing.

PEACE #2

Last night, at sunset, deepest purples,
magentas, violets; streaked earth, water,
sky—sun on fire—mind on fire—

heart on fire—womb on fire—
and the Crescent cooled me, the Whole
in shadow—someone built an immense

sandcastle surrounded by star
fish, each pinnacle crowned by
a soft, white feather—I whispered,

"On Earth as it is in Heaven,
in Heaven as it is on Earth—give
the lovers peace, give them starfish

and white feathers." I thought
of you, Rainbow Bird,
my Mango.

Love is the sandcastle.
Peace is the tide.
The sun is on fire.

The whole in shadow.

PEACE #3

Is this peace? Kayaking through
the water with a man I do not
love.

Is this peace? Watching a well-fed,
fearless, white-headed otter spin in
seaweed.

Is this peace? Breathing softly as steel
gray pelicans blend and swoop through
fog.

Is this peace? Sitting at sunset with
my nine-year-old son making up nonsense words,
laughing.

Is this peace? The fierce, dark owl perched
on a branch, the horizon burns as she
plunges.

Is this peace? Wondering if it's love, or the lack
of it, that ceases to desire what I do not
possess.

PEACE #4

I dream an actress making love

to a man, and though she

doesn't love him, he says

the right words—an old sorrow,

an old passion, an old love

fills her—I hear the words,

"She desires to love

and not to hate."

And I am filled with admiration

for this actress—she also knows

peace. Is this actress me,

Mango?

PEACE #5

Mango,
It no longer makes me sad,
nor do I rush to remove
the naked rose from water,
purple petals scattered
everywhere—little seeds,
rose hips, hips of the rose,
gather and swell—fertile,
abundant. Worlds without
end. I gaze at the naked
flower, its empty beauty—
so many petals, each one a
rose.

PEACE #6

Dolphins dancing before me—

the headlines read: "MORE TROOPS

SHIPPED, BUSH STANDS FIRM"—

my car runs on oil, yes, our

world runs on oil, but, I think,

couldn't everything run, work

with our sun, turning sun into

the Great Lover of Earth, rather

than the Great Destroyer (the

greenhouse effect)—yes, they danced.

A dolphin, YES, she said,

dancing, twirling, high in the air—

the sun turning her body into

rainbows. (I dreamt a dolphin

swam up to me last night and told

me she loved me with her smooth, rainbow

skin touching mine.)

And you, Mango, with

your rainbow

feathers.

PEACE #7

I must confess, Mango,
I hesitated to water the almost
dead plant, thinking, What's
the use? The forlorn leaves,
sky gathering rain (the
bones of heaven become brittle;
the Earth stretches, drought,
earthquake, tornado): I water
the pale, green leaves, your wise
bird's voice whispering, "All of
life cannot be of use to you—
all of life cannot be of use to you."
Earth and sky,
onebody.

MIND (PEACE #8)

I rest in high tide,

in the rainbows

of the world—

spring rises, sweetly,

in the sun's light,

and rises, again, by

soothing moonlight—

my mind is free to wander—

my mind is free to rest—

at the center of the world

is a motherless baby, created

from all flesh, all blood—

s/he thrives on air, light, leftover

love—

at the center of the world, Mango,

is a motherless baby who

dreams and wakens

wakens and dreams.

From a dream—

PEACE #9

In the soaring light,

The Earth greets her lover—

Wind, clouds, mountains, rain—

Why does it come to this,

The Earth receiving life,

The Earth creating life—

(Mango knows, singing—)

Humans and our daily stupidities;

The molecules of Paradise

Embedded in my cunt, my melting

Womb—

There is peace in the body/mind—

The molecules of Paradise, within

Us, this Earth, the soaring, singing

Light.

PEACE #10

In the middle of anger, tears,
a familiar despair; as the car

warmed up, I glanced at my house
once more, and the shadow of

a small, brown thrush calmed
me:

"I bring you death, I bring you silence,

I bring you old loves, I bring you new loves,

I am pausing for you.

I do not sing."

And she didn't sing. She was absolutely

still, calm, still.

She knew she held *forever and ever*

in frail bone, bird blood, each feather.

You birds are so wise, Mango—

your shadows in the bright winter

sun.

       *   *   *

Who really loves me?

Can I count them on one hand?

And when they cease to love me,

do my fingers fall off?

No. But my heart is not the same.

Some sweetness lost, dripping into

my body. I should not tilt, but

hold it: still, calm, still.

*   *   *

I tell my children stories about
their childhood, still—30, 28, 24.

I love to tell the stories, they love
to hear about themselves, better than

a video, *what they were to me: mine.*
This morning I realized my mother never tells

me stories about my childhood (my grandmother
would've, but she turned into air); so, naturally,

I became a writer so I wouldn't disappear,
so *I would matter: mine.* And I love to

read other's stories, that they saw
a blue sky one morning and dew on the fresh

earth and nothing, nothing mattered but
this joy. A small bird's shadow.

*   *   *

Mango, be wise for me—

when the familiar despair leaps up

and I must fight and spit, tell me,

"You are more than the sum of your

parts; you are capable of loving

even the air, what doesn't matter."

*   *   *

I turn my body toward the sun.

I love my sharp/edged winter shadow.

December 1990

PEACE #11

A friend brings me a carved jade,
ornate, circle within a circle, and it
defies logic; how did they do it—
carve a circle within a circle;
this person must be a master of peace:
someone chained to a wall by the neck—
someone who must carve for a bowl of rice—
someone dying, being put to use—
someone so young she doesn't matter—
someone sitting on a mountain listening to
the wind, the silence of her soul, watching
clouds part, eagles hunt, and her fingers
know the circle within the circle; her secret
she sells for pennies; they advertise on TV
for millions of dollars with full guarantees.
I'll take the circle within the circle
and defy logic, Mango.
I'll take no guarantees.
Peace.

PEACE #12

Mango,
they rattle their swords;
the children wear gas masks
   (chemical warfare, no, never, ever);
women soldiers kiss their daughters goodbye;
they prepare for war to make peace;
the young may die again;
they die for old men's failing dreams;
they die for the god oil;
the old Goddess, Sun, shines too harshly;
she shines madly;
she waits for soft, yellow sanity;
she wishes to give us wildflowers, corn, oats,
sweet rivers, thunder and rain;
peace.
May the Old One bring sanity.
May the Old One bring sanity.

Now,

Mango.

PEACE #13

They're ordering 80,000 body bags
for our young in the Persian Gulf,

and that's just to start, I'm sure.
Did 80,000 mothers give birth to

death? Our government pumps our money
to the dictators of the world, and we're

supposed to believe we're free
because we can haggle about abstractions,

because I can write this poem that
says our government is fucked and

all the fucking letters I've written
weren't worth the stamp I licked on them

because they're ordering the body bags
after giving Saddam Hussein $1.5 billion

to develop the weapons that will kill
our young, and as I write this poem

I know it lacks grace, beauty, style,
but who will read it anyway, or take it

seriously in this country, in this time—
Mango, murder is sanctioned. War is

peace. Fuck the body bags: show me
each wound, the missing face and hands:

bring each one, an offering to Bush:
lay them before his feet and have

that mother recount her labor and favorite
childhood stories, each one: if the face

is gone, let her describe the face,
in detail: if the hand is gone, let her

tell of touch: fuck the body bags.
I want to remember

peace.
I do remember

peace.
The whole, living body.

The sanctity of life.
I want to look at it.

I want to touch it, so
p e a c e f u l l y

WAR

My womb is aching,

            Mango,

in sympathy with each woman's
dying child, and the women who
die with their children, and the
women who kill, cradling death
in their wombs, their scorched arms,
the men who kill the child without,
within.

My womb is aching

            Mango,

but it will heal.

I will wear the mask

of she-who-gives-birth-in-spite-of

logic: she/god, she/dog,

she/wolf. She who eats the darkness

and lights the way.

CELEBRATION

I cannot be bothered with war
and death in spring (men declare
    a killing time, sending the young,
    again, to die, and though the Earth
    has suffered from man's stupidity,
    it simply is her way to bloom,
    again, to bring life from the barren
    tree, the silent forest, the frozen
    ground—it is her way, to bloom—
    she, the Goddess, doesn't believe
    in war or death, only in fertilizer,
    food for the living, preparation
    for the new, ripening of the old,
    transformation, re-birth, the re-cycling
    of the human soul, the beauty
    of the body, its brief, vivid
    glory). Spring is the celebration

of death through life. Remember.

PERENNIAL

Well, Mango, my song has
been muted by sorrow—

I was thinking of war, loss of love,
death, the bombing of little children

in Baghdad, the families that go to sleep
waiting for the bombs to drop, the one

that may just find them, the mother,
weeping, holding her small child,

the young soldiers, both sides,
18, 19, 20, 21, 22, yes, dead.

My heart filled up with too much
sorrow, dread and sorrow (though,

    of course, spring has come, again,
    making me love her); it began to ache

and scream. So, now, I let the sunset
colors soothe me—there will be peace,

again, and pregnant women and loving men.
The young will blossom from the gnarled,

seemingly dead bush like fresh
roses.

ORCHIDS AND COMETS
AS I APPROACH
50

10 perfect orchids bloom
in the still winter-light—

outside spring greets me,
flirtatious as a teenager

in heat—inside, on my
kitchen table, are these 10

perfect orchids nurtured
by wind and storm—orchids

are not teenagers, but fully
grown, inviting, wise, luxuriously

sexual, their heat cool as
comets.

       ★   ★   ★

They say a shell of 100 billion
comets surrounds the solar system,

their tails as long as 100 million
miles when they flare from the

solar wind—sometimes a passing
star will nudge one toward the sun—

in lieu of seeing 100 billion comets,
I'm content to see these 10 perfect

orchids, blossomed, each one, with
no apologies to moon

or sun.

INSTINCT

First, I dreamt the Spirit
Of The House telling me how
dissatisfied she is with death,
her death, and how the dying

is perpetual and unending, and how
she died (again), and how death
happens when some aren't ready.
I woke sad and frightened; all these

secrets I prefer not to know (but
preference has never been my friend,
only *You must, You will)*, and I
looked out at the 4 am stars,

Hour of My Wolf. A lone bird called
as I've never, ever, heard before—
two clear, short bursts—a signal.
Frozen with terror, I didn't want to

open the garden door, but I did,
(*You must, You will),* and the
bird burst into song; I could hear
the ocean in the street taking mailboxes,

cars, lawns, the artifacts of civilization;
I smiled with delight, prepared to meet
my Wolf, my Death. The air was sweet
and lonely, and I was all-one (alone)

in the world, not by preference, but
I must, I will. I opened the bedroom
window wider; cold tongues licked
my willing flesh, and as I dove

into the dream I asked, "Spirit
Of The House, why are you so
fond of dying?" In the dream,
my blankets were trying to kill me

as I faced the hungry dark.
The dark had no pity, no words
of consolation: nothing: then
I knew. I began to make love

to myself, lowering the blankets,
bit by bit, exposing my self to
the hungry dark, until I married
it (again) and fed myself. Completely,

yes, completely satisfied with
the hungry dark. First Lover,
Awful Bliss and Ecstasy, *I will
not live without you.*

My Dream, March 1993

BLUE MOON NIGHT

Young men on a rock, facing
 the sea on a Blue Moon
night, howl like wolves

and laugh. They give me
hope that there are men
who sing their souls

like wolves, like fools,
and love the Blue Moon,
her roses that open only

to the voice
of sweet, sweet
surrender.

                    ★   ★   ★

Further down the beach,
a young man plays a soft, soft
guitar that sings

so sweetly, so sweetly,
to the roses in my
womb.

These are the blood-red roses
of infinite tenderness, with
the scent of Creation.

In order to create, one
must surrender, so sweetly,
so sweetly, to the awe full

mystery. To the Blue Moon
night that is not
blue at all.

"Instead of trying to become buddha,
you suddenly realize that buddha is
trying to become you."
—Chögyam Trungpa, *Crazy Wisdom*

MY BUDDHA

The other night, before sleep,
I said, at last, "I may never

know what love is with
a man, that meeting, that getting

to the bottom of it, beyond
ego, survival, power, fear—"

It seems when you do go beyond
ego, survival, power, fear,

you reach the essence of what
is there: cruelty   compassion.

There are those that say a soft cruelty
is preferable to a hard compassion.

Since I'm not truly civilized,
I cannot say.

        ⋆   ⋆   ⋆

I dream a youthful man in his fifties—
he's rich, he tells me, as he drives

the car, playfully—I'm giving
him directions through my childhood

city (San Francisco)—I do not trust
him, but I find him humorous,

a pleasure—we come to the top of an extremely
steep hill (I hope his brakes work)—

at the bottom, there appears
to be a dead end (for a moment,

   I'm disappointed)—then, I see
a giant Buddha at the bottom of the steep

hill and that cars are leaving, one by one,
through a gateway—the man looks at me

and laughs with delight—I trust
him, yes, I trust him—I kiss

him on the cheek, this man, rich
with my Buddha.

CENTER

I brought home a bunch of multi
colored roses: pink, peach, red,

and when I set them free,
six were beheaded, stem from

fresh, young bud. At first,
I was angry, disappointed.

Then, a wiser voice, from my center,
told me what to do: a shallow

bowl of water, place them
in a circle, watch the circle

bloom. The roses think themselves
perfect.

HOW THE WISE WOMAN LAUGHS IN ME, NOW

I'm at the age (forty-nine),
I realize, that
when a man exposes his genitals

to me, I have to laugh—
the tap, tap, tapping behind
me, on a garbage can, I think;

I, facing the rising-sun-sea,
watching for something truly
exciting; a young, dark seal—

I turn and glance—he thinks
he's broken the last taboo—
he thinks he's shocked me—

yes, he thinks I am frightened
as I burst into unrestrained
laughter—poor man, it's so tiny,

so shriveled, it shrinks before
the rising sun (now, don't get
me wrong; if a lovely man, naked,

unaware of game or role or power play,
walked by, I'd look, I'd admire
his relaxed, dangling penis, his muscled

hips and thighs, the well-built legs,
up to the flare of belly, sweet hair,
the chest, the man-nipples erect in the

chill morning air, the fine, long
neck, the chin, the eyes that see,
the lips that taste, smile, the indifferent

masculine back as he walks away—I
love backs—the chest says *hello,*
the back says *goodbye*—the buttocks,

buttocks to both sexes, how they float
and glide, and let me imagine
anything). I'm at the age

when I accept the task of pulling
the wet-birthed petals from the pod,
the Birds of Paradise,

without a whimper; place
their wetness to my forehead;
it's my job to see

the mundane, the miracle.
I take hold of it with my
hands and make beauty.

First Words

A friend, a painter,
tells me: "I see you

dancing on the very tip
of a flame." Her eyes smile

as her fingers move in a dance
like fire, and I laugh with

recognition, with the dread
and desire of that dance

which leaves me so alone . . .
my fear and ecstasy.

It is the dance of Creation,
sometimes shared, often alone;

when I fall, fall, fall into
the fire and die (in ecstasy)

only to be reborn . . .
something so *new*,

so strange, I wonder
what I'll say.

à la Carmen

TIME

First, I had to love the world
as a poet, and only then
could I write the *facts*,
the daily exchange of petty

survival (and its ration
    of miracles; the fact that
the sun rises, later the moon,
and the stars appear, one

by one); I had to give
birth four times—one
daughter, three sons—
    in order to love the human

race; I had to belong
to this and to that, to know
    I belong to no one
but the Universe, our

human stories, unwinding
from Her Womb; I make
    myself small and hungry—
I enter like a child and

listen quietly, raptly, to
the world, the many voices
out there, and the Universe
    carries me, carries me,

    as I listen and write,
listen and write, crouched
and warm, fed, where I belong
(I sigh at the loneliness,

at the fullness of my place,
here at the center, at the very
    center of the Universe), listening
to time unfold.

In honor of prose—

MEMORY

I dream you, Bob,
for the first time since
your death, your transformation—

I imagine you, hurled headlong
back into someone's womb,
greedily suckling darkness, remembering

the sound of the Universe, Her
Heart, as blood and translucence
fill your delicate fetal cells,

your sweet, thin eyelids trembling,
trying to dream your life and why
you died so suddenly, and why

the pain of living was so hard,
as ecstasy ebbs and peaks, each wave,
through your newly created body.

But in the dream you came as you
were, as I knew you, just to be my
friend, just to say you loved me

and that I was not to forget.
We joked and laughed; you were
light, playful, as I saw you from

time to time. I assume you're trying
to tell me we're the culmination of everyone
and everything we've ever loved, and that

nothing is ever, ever lost, only
added to the great memory of Creation.
I see your head in the Circle of Blood—

I see your new-born face in light—
I hear your startled, angry cry—
How could I ever forget you?

To Bob Ross, M.D.

EARLY MORNING, DECEMBER 25TH, 1994

Orchids in full bloom (delicate
   creams, pinks, purples, golden

genital-centers), to the left, in the
garden. Beyond, yellow sun-hearted

daisies, and, beyond, comet-throated
African daisies. The tree my 28-year-old

son and I planted during an argument
grows full, so full, straight-spined,

immense (tiny yellow-tipped sparrows
   nest in its supple branches).

To my right an Eagle Kachina dances,
its red beak open, singing to the Sun.

(My grandmother used to sing
to the rising and setting Sun

in the tongue of her people,
the undefeated Yaqui.

My grandmother, when she was
angry, or a passion filled

her, looked like an eagle—
clear, far-seeing, focused on her

   prey.) Mi mamacita (my grandmother)
and my grandfather (Jesús y Pablo) marry

each other (in a photo next to the
   Eagle), 1906, nearly 90 years ago

in Sonora, Mexico (how lovely she
   is in white white lace; she

carries asters, lilies, roses; her
   eyes guard her joy well; instead,

I see duty, loyalty, destiny;
and on her innocent, wise

head is her veil, her crown).
Outside, by my mailbox, the Birds

of Paradise are in full bloom,
spiky-tipped, orange and purple.

Flung from a farther star,
willing their roots into

this planet, this Earth,
this paradise,

they whisper,
they shout,

"The gifts are coming,
the gifts are coming . . ."

(90 years later
their grandchild accepts

their gifts of
destiny.)

To my grandmother, Jesús,
an unpublished poet—
To my grandfather, Pablo,
a published poet.

Santa Cruz, California,
edge of the continent

"Power is being told you are not loved and
not being destroyed by it."
—Madonna, "The Madonna Diaries"

"I AM NOT IN LOVE WITH YOU," he said

The storm outside is clearing dead
tree limbs, leaves, clouds—
readying us for spring.

The storm inside is clearing false
flesh words, hearts, eyes—
readying us for spring.

I am a woman who has held
my ground, mountain-lion growl,
continuing my walk to the peaks.

I am a woman who has shoveled
snow, starting over my head, down
to my feet, and laughing.

I am a woman who has held the pain
of childbirth four times between my
teeth, severed the cord, joyfully.

I am a woman who has pulled porcupine
quills from my beloved dog's lips, held
him three years later as he died.

I am a woman who felt a moth melt into
my right ear, to hear the voices clearly,
and I am not insane, in fact too sane.

I am a woman who was the wall for raging
sons, no father, refusing to let them
go, I held held held held, then let go.

I am a woman whose daughter is not
me, she is someone else, someone
foreign, surprising, infuriating, mine.

I am a woman who killed my father's cancer
pain, whispered to his angry, stubborn spirit,
"Go to the light, Father, to the light, now."

I am a woman whose love
for her mother was never
simply received.

I am the daughter of a woman, struggling
with old age, who looks me in the eyes:
"I love life, I love every damn day."

I am a woman who's cleaned puke, diarrhea,
maggots, trusting the source: delicate green
shoots, hands of lust, a multitude, conceiving.

I am a woman who wanted to create the
world with you, daily, from
desire.

Once in the mountains, in my solitary cabin,
my wolf-dog (Sirius) brought me a skull
at the back door, an immense thigh

bone at the front door; surrounded by
death I was fearful, grateful, knowing
the gifts were coming through the terrible

difficult gateway, birth canal, Vagina
of the Universe (pain/joy pain/joy pain/joy).
And though you've placed your death

at my front and back door, and I stand
at the center without your love, I am
not unloved. I am just being born.

Newly born.
This spring.
In love.

I must create
the world my
self.

In January

DEAR WORLD (Words)

January 10, 1994

DEAR WORLD,

A photo of myself at sixteen,
my daughter maybe six months
old—black sweater, some
exotic yellow lacquered fruit,
in uneven slices, around my neck,
held by a thick chain (strange

   but beautiful)—my hair
so short, my mouth painted
white, so firm, holding its
pain, silently—but the eyes,
yes, the eyes, edged in black
all around, are fearless,
determined to see as clearly
as possible, to remember
my daughter's smile, even her
screaming, angry face—
I see my grandmother's
eyes, and my great-grandmother's
eyes, and probably my great-
great-grandmother's eyes, and
I love this fearless girl/woman—
she had so far to go before

the white, silent mouth

became red and spoke her simple

truth—and I remember when

I saw this photo at sixteen and

thought I didn't look like

other girls, *not pretty,*

but strange like the lacquered

fruit at my throat—

I remember now, at forty-nine, that

I thought I was ugly,

and I see, now, that

I was beautiful, so beautiful,

like the warrior women

of old. And wise.

But never, ever,

pretty. In my forty-ninth year,

nearly fifty, I can say that

I love you (I am scarred

   from many battles—raped,

punched, knocked down, re

fusing to stay down, sub

missive) I love you,

dear World.

Dear World,

I come to the edge of
the world at 8:10 am

to see if the tide is
high or low,

to see if the sun is
rising in winter,

to see if ducks, wild ones,
still love the sky;

and the tide is high,
wild, striking cliffs

with rainbows, daily
gifts from the sun—

on the other side of
the world, people must

run in the streets, holding
their children's hands, hoping

the sniper will miss—
the old, the slow,

are killed, and no one
can touch the body

or they, too, will die—
a woman, my age, stands

on a road, her vigil, throwing
stones at trucks, full of

children, women like herself,
the old, screaming, YOU KILLED

MY BOY! YOU KILLED, YOU KILLED
MY BOY! Her boy, one year

younger than my son,
tortured, killed, made

to dig his own grave—
you see, my Earth,

I'm grateful for my life,
this magnificent world I've

come to witness—but I must
weigh her life

and mine,
daily.

The killing in Bosnia—

DEAR WORLD,

Winter approaches in the spring
blossoms by the back fence:
bright, vivid fuchsia (like
    wild roses) with yellow centers
from the Sun sing winter's
praises. They must *visibly*
die for spring's emergence—
if it (spring) looks alive, it won't
work—it (winter) must be
DEAD   DEAD   DEAD.
Only then can the miracle
occur (in Los Angeles/The Angels,
the Earth danced, her hips
swaying with abandon—
do we imagine she is not
alive? She is frightening
in her dance; one foot
death, one foot life,
dancing with the Sun, Moon,
Stars and every Planet
in the Cosmos).
Dear World,
miracles are terrible
and wonderful in their
mystery.
Without the dance,
nothing (so says
Ixchel,
the wanderer).

                    Santa Cruz, winter/spring

January 26, 1994

DEAR WORLD,

Children in Bosnia ran out to
play in the glittering light snow,

in war, in a time of war
(did the soldiers see

them sledding, running,
playing in the light—

did they see themselves
as children playing

in the light—
did they realize,

did they know, they
were killing their own,

their very *own* child's
soul that must be, is

drawn, irresistibly, even
in war, to play, to always

play in the light);
and they died, bombed

by men who should've been
their fathers, brothers, uncles,

grandfathers. Witnesses said, "The
 snow was covered with blood."

The glittering light snow
is covered with blood.

A child's head lies
separate, startled,

from its perfect
body.

A witness (me) says,
"Bow our own heads. *See*

the child playing in the light."

DEAR WORLD,

My orchid plant gave me a long

stem of orchids, ten are

in bloom (white fleshy petals,

purple genitals, a yellow

tongue); if I were a painter,

I'd start with the petals,

like a striptease, only

adding as I go—petal by

petal, the whole; if I were

a painter, the final orchid

would return to the rain

forests, to the south,

and, magically, through

the sheer force of beauty,

erupting from the mind

and will of Earth herself,

the orchid would grant

Native Peoples the land

required for food, life,

orchids.

*A la gente de
Tepeyac, México*

February 11, 1994

DEAR WORLD,

Every morning a mockingbird,
so fat and healthy,

comes to sit in the branches
of my tree, and while it

sits, mostly it's silent
    (why is it that certain

men want to kill the Soul
of the World . . . they want

to kill young girls, their
bodies, their spirits . . . I

read in the newspaper that three
12 year olds and one 13 year old

screamed, kicked, fought back . . .
they were not silent, and

escaped . . . I tell my 13-year-old
son, "If you're ever threatened,

even with a knife or gun, fight
back, yell, better to die fighting

on your spot than be taken,
tortured, killed" . . . a terrible

thing to tell our children—girls,
boys—but true; be warriors, I

tell you, and save the Soul of the
World); and when it flies

it sings.

DEAR WORLD,

The grandmothers cross the Bridge
of Brotherhood and Unity in Sarajevo
today—a young soldier, his
M-16 lowered, bulletproof
vest, ammo in his pockets,
steel helmet on his head,
pushes barbed wire to the
side, respectfully, as a
grandmother, unarmed, struggles
to lift her baggage, eyes
to the ground (they do not
allow "males of fighting age"—
11 to 70?—to cross, only
the grandmothers may cross).
Now, she is crossing the Bridge
of Grandmother's Wisdom, counting
the dead like birds in the morning
sky; counting the living
like flowers in the spring
wind;
silently, persistently, fiercely,
secretly (she remembers everything,
her eyes to the
ground).

Dear World,

As a child I knew spring

by its sunlight, the way

my eyes wanted more;

it was like thirst

or hunger; so, what I was

given I took, and what

I lacked I stole. Sun

light, spring, were free;

so, I thought I was rich,

rich with the sun,

and that the sun, spring,

and I had no beginning.

No ending.

This,

I knew as a child.

DEAR WORLD,

I stand on the wet edge

of the tide,

of the sea,

of the continent,

California,

and I see

the people of Africa slaughtering

one another,

the people of Bosnia slaughtering

one another,

the inner cities of the United

States, border to border,

the people of China, Turkey,

Mexico, Central America, Brazil,

Korea, Thailand, Tibet, Israel,

Arabia, Palestine, Ireland,

border to border to border,

and I stand at the wet edge

of the world in

California;

I gaze at my iridescent

shadow, glittering with gold,

the sweet hiss of tide,

Mother of us all,

the only true borders,

Her Womb, the land masses

One, once. I remember

when this continent kissed

the circle of time,

and how we survived.

And how we survived.

DEAR WORLD,

Today, early this morning,
I saw a great blue heron

sipping light—to my right,
a shy rainbow read my

thoughts, arching further into
Earth and Sky—and the ocean

committed suicide, repeatedly,
before it withdrew to give

birth, again, to plain salt—
and the salt made me

smile/laugh/weep/dream
(one grain, I knew, and

I would be immortal—
I would leave this woman's

body, not to enter the human
body for eternity; instead,

I would *be* light, bringing
rainbows, shadows;

I would quench the thirst
of the great blue heron).

And with plain salt, and light,
I would take part in the process

of destruction, and
creation.

July 15, 1994

DEAR WORLD,

A mockingbird perches at
the very tip of the pine

tree my 28-year-old son
and I planted (I take it

   he wishes to greet me,
my son in Europe right now).

In Paris, German troops
return 50 years after

the year of my birth,
a gesture of healing

(so many dead
so many dead).

May it be true,
Dear World,

that my son sings from
a mockingbird's throat;

that we are healing
in my 50th year.

DEAR WORLD, WHY?

The dark, shimmering strands
of light   color   hang
from my tree; the last
light of my Sun plays
with its brooding
rainbows. I think
of love   hate
sorrow   joy . . .

Why would a soldier
kill a boy, pluck
out his eye like
a rose, then give
the boy to his
mother? Why?

I think of my 14-year-
old son, old enough
to be killed in Bosnia.
I think of his eyes
blossoming in his beloved face.
I think of my roses
blossoming in the garden.

Life is good, yes,
life is good
where strands of rainbows
sway in the twilight
wind and soldiers
do   not   pluck
my   roses.

DEAR WORLD,

Does Love feed the hungry?

Does Love ripen slowly?

Or bloom suddenly one morning?

Or sway in the dark wind?

Does Love swell like a pumpkin?

Is Love a thin, dark root?

Is Love the harvest?

Or the wind-borne seed?

Is Love translucent tears from the sky?

Is Love virgin snow?

Is Love a virgin?

Is Love a whore?

I am a virgin and

a whore, consumed by

your PRESENCE

          *   *   *

And I am alone

in this world surrounded

by so many people

that love me,

that hate me,

yet, I am alone

with you,

Love

⋆   ⋆   ⋆

Are you the newborn seeking darkness?
Are you the dying seeking light?
Are you my left hand?
And my right?
Are you my body carrying
me through this life
time?

⋆   ⋆   ⋆

Are you this presence?

DEAR WORLD,

I stand under an open

sky as the Cosmos

shifts—planets

rotate, stars die

in their million-year

cycles, comets blaze

the Void, seeking fusion,

explosion, a resting

place—newly born

stars roar with light,

neither proud nor frightened,

they exist to burn,

to fill the Void with song—

I listen.

The moon throws her cold,

wise light across the

human spectrum, history,

as I sit with warm sake,

unglazed clay in my hand,

dug from the Earth,

my sweet sweet Earth,

to feed me at 4:18 am

in the morning, as you

dream/wake, World, and I

witness the Cosmos shift,

undisturbed, serene, inhumanly

peace full,

I am your

human gazing

up

Dear World,

Fifty journeys around the
Sun—
Fifty journeys around the
Sun—
I am fifty today,
my lamp held high,
I gaze at you, World,
between bouts of rain,
wind, sun, rainbows,
rain to cleanse my
vision
that I may see
what is.
Fifty journeys around the
Sun.

          ★   ★   ★

At night:
Thunder   Lightning   Rain
Stars streak across
the sky in my dreams.
In my dreams, I fall
in love for the first

time, always for

the first time, sweet

innocence, passion,

my own

DESIRE.

Dangerous, necessary, as

Thunder   Lightning   Rain

(O innocence, O Moon,

O Sun of my

own Universe in my

50th year).

In gratitude to the Earth,
who gave me all of her
gifts in one day—

DEAR WORLD,

Your ways are messy,
people dying all the time—

the 19-year-old Israeli soldier
shot by his captors, an

8-month-old girl beaten to death
by her mother's boyfriend,

a 5 year old dropped from
14 floors in Chicago because

he wouldn't steal candy for
10 year olds; the endless

slaughter of wars—on TV
grown men admit to killing

children in Rwanda; Bosnia
continues its killing, as well

as China (in Tibet), Latin America . . .
I planted lotus in cold murky water;

the round leaves float
hopefully to the top.

This, I've heard: "From
the darkness and the mud

the perfect lotus lily
blooms."

DEAR WORLD,

A photograph of President Clinton,
have you seen it . . . walking
with soldiers in Germany
before they leave for Bosnia—

his face stark, alone,
the face of a man trained
not to weep (but he does
anyway): "We cannot stop

all war for all time, but
we can stop some wars.
We cannot save all women
and children, but we can save

many of them. We can't do
everything, but we must do
what we can . . . The terrible
war in Bosnia is such a case."

I am a woman who despises
the *machinery of war,* the endless,
nameless, faceless massacres of
nations; and I am a woman

sick in my soul, hearing
the stories of the dead
children, the rape of women,
the torture of men,

the innocent dead,
the innocent dead.
And I am proud that my
president wants to weep.

March 24, 1996

Dear World,

18,400 years ago, this comet
we call (in 1996) Hyakutake
came close to the Earth (10 million
miles away, 10 million); but we

can see it with the naked
eye, floating in the sky like
a tail of light. The last
time it came within 10 million

miles, humans were just crossing
the terrible, icy glaciers,
the Bering Strait, into this
land mass, North America, one

of the floating, enduring Turtles.
The Turtles whispered, "Leap of
faith, dream, leap of faith, dream,"
as the comet edged its way

10 million miles, so close. 18,400
years later, the Turtles whisper,
"Leap of faith, one planet, leap
of faith, one people," This planet

floating through the stars, comets
coming home to sing to the Turtles:
"Cross the terrible, icy glaciers,
the human heart, leap."

(I sent the December 3, 1995, poem to President Clinton and received a warm response from him. Now I must send this one.)

August 12, 1996

DEAR PRESIDENT CLINTON,

Imagine you're a small boy,
maybe four, your mother
is alone, no husband,
you have no father,

you have no supportive
relatives, she must
find a way to survive,
to feed and clothe you,

there is no day care,
you live in a project
where other children die
of stray bullets, daily,

you may be dead by five
and your mother loves you,
but she can't protect
you, barely feed you,

you are the youngest of
five, you will never be
President, but you will know
hunger and fear, intimately—

Imagine, a president who
takes away even the hunger
and fear (AFDC 1% of federal budget)—
How would the president eat without

swallowing the hunger and fear
of millions of children—how would
the president take his vitamins while
millions of children slowly/quietly starve—

Imagine, you're a mother praying
for mercy, working as hard as you
humanly can to keep your children
fed and clean (powdered milk, rationed,

peanut butter a luxury, clothes budget
of $5 per child at the 2nd hand, never a new
bike). I've been on welfare with three
children in my early twenties (when I left

their father, he never paid me a dime),
and I hated it, but I needed it for
less than a year. Me, I'm too angry
to be the sacrificial lamb at the altar

of our national abundance; those bleeding
lambs make our (the fed) lives possible;
we don't even bother to honor their still
beating hearts to the rising sun. Imagine.

THE WORK OF LOVE

THE WORK OF LOVE, UNFOLDING

All I have is twenty crickets.
All I have is twenty crickets
that I bought for five cents

each at the pet store,
and I set them free
in my yard. One I heard

making song. One I saw
in my wastebasket. That
leaves eighteen for pure

good luck. And I
need it. A dollar's
worth of luck.

                          *   *   *

Cricket #1 for song.
Cricket #2 for company.
Cricket #3 for the neighbors.
Cricket #4 for sunlight.
Cricket #5 for starlight.
Cricket #6 for the waning moon.
Cricket #7 for the mockingbirds.
Cricket #8 for the children.
Cricket #9 for the raped women/girls of Bosnia.
Cricket #10 for the unborn.
Cricket #11 for the Unfolding of our species.
Cricket #12 for the starving.
Cricket #13 for the Goddess.
Cricket #14 for the God.
Cricket #15 for the newly born.
Cricket #16 for purity, innocence, godinthesoul.
Cricket #17 for all warriors with wombs.
Cricket #18 for their children.
Cricket #19 for their fathers.
Cricket #20 for the rainbow,

that we may have eyes to see
all the colors of the spectrum—

that we may have ears to hear
all the cries of sorrow/joy: the voices—

that we may have hands to touch
the gentle and stop the ungentle—

that we may have feet to flee, hunt,
fight and dance upon this fiercely tender

Earth.

$$\star \qquad \star \qquad \star$$

I do not believe we are doomed to des
truction, dis aster (separation from
the stars, an unforeseen calamity)—

I believe we see it clearly,
whether we are being pulled from
our houses, raped, shot, imprisoned,

or simply starving, or buying bright
yellow parakeets for our children,
or feeding the wild birds, or carrying

signs saying HOMELESS, PLEASE HELP,
or mourning the loss of love, or celebrating
love's First Face, never lost, never found,

watching us with infinite, inhuman
wisdom (we think we've found it one more
time); and from that clarity, we know

the work of love, the Unfolding of our
species, is woven in the light of every
star, in the span of centuries, our

souls stretching out and out,
a delicately enduring spider's web
the size of the Universe, catching light,

catching souls, holding the dark,
lovers and enemies created, oh so clearly,
by the hardest work, by the guilty

who return newly born, pure with godinthesoul,
who will, with some luck, in time, not forget.
Re member.

To the children
with godintheeyes,
my guides, always—
(And to my son Jules at 15.)

THE GUEST

The wind has broken down
the door of my heart,
and my heart hangs open, open;
the small, dazzling bird

that used to sing just for
me, just for me,
has escaped the cage
of my heart, and now

I hear the small, dazzling
bird singing from roof
tops, faraway branches,
dancing with colorful kites,

racing clouds at sunrise,
resting her wings at sunset,
and singing, singing to the World,
and singing, singing to the Cosmos

my secret heart-songs of
sorrow and fury and great
joy. I listen to my bird
and my heart is wide open

as the wind blows through
as the wind blows through
the cage of my broken heart,
and I am grateful she escaped

and she now sings to all
who listen. Yes, my heart
is broken (what *pain*,
what *pain*)—but I never,

not ever, wanted to
keep the small, dazzling
bird a prisoner of my heart.
I prefer to hear her singing

to the World, to the Cosmos,
my secret heart-songs,
and the door of the cage is wide
open. She may return and rest

and listen to my new songs, then
lift her wings when her time
has come to leave, when
her time has come to leave

my heart, the cage of my broken
heart, and fly free to sing
to all who listen. This pain.
This wind. Has set her free.

Now I *see* the small, dazzling
bird; I had no idea she was
this beautiful, this prisoner
of my heart (is free). What

strange, strange joy
this empty heart,
this broken heart,
this small, dazzling bird,

free to leave,
free to return.
What pain, what strange
joy to always welcome you,

my bird, not as the prisoner
of my childhood heart,
but as the guest of
my heart's wisdom.

April 1997, Santa Cruz

*To my lovebird Mango, who left his
rainbow body as I held him to my
heart in the sun's light.*

146

UNDER VENUS

I am the lover.
I am the loved.

Is this true?
Can I believe that?

I ask myself buying
a star necklace and star earrings

for my daughter's birth
day 37 years ago.

I am the lover.
I am the loved.

I choose a crystal
heart for my daughter-

in-law's graduation
and playful cards for friends.

I am the lover.
I am the loved.

I buy Power Bars for
my 16-year-old son

and champagne for my son-
in-law's birthday.

I am the lover.
I am the loved.

I think of a student's
story, the one we talked

about last summer, her
fear of writing it, she

wrote through her fear
to magic, to love.

I am the lover.
I am the loved.

(At the beach)
I see a young father
playing with his tiny

son on the sand,
he crouches and when

his son leaps, he
falls, both in ecstasy.

I am the lover.
I am the loved.

The tiny blond son looks
like my 30-year-old son

27 years ago; the young
father looks like my

34-year-old son now;
so I smile and weep

as they play and fall,
play and fall in ecstasy.

I am the lover,
I am the loved.

(At home)
I am the lover.
I am the loved.

My 16-year-old son is
in pain because his father

has gone from his home,
his daily life, leaving

him to mourn a loss
as boy becomes man;

leaving him to me, seeking
his Fountain of Youth

somewhere else (he turned
   50 last year). This

year I am 53; I see
my Fountain of Youth in

my son's eyes, in the
eyes of children, in the

eyes of the lover
and the loved.

I gaze deeply.
I see the truth.

I am the lover.
I am the loved.

               ★   ★   ★

I watch my 16-year-old
son and his first girl

friend wrestle with water
bottles, run into the house

drenched, eat pizza to
gether, study together,

laugh together; young sweet
hearts, they break my heart,

their innocence, first love.
I'm not jealous or envious,

just watchful (this is my
   job, isn't it?) As I walk

past my son's room
I see them resting in

each other's arms, two
tired children under Venus,

her bright, unwavering light;
two tired children trusting

Venus, and I am watchful,
and I remember

I am the lover.
I am the loved.

(Morning Star)
We tilt toward the Sun,
I spill from dreams.

Last night I laughed in
my dreams. Last night

I wept in my dreams.
Last night I knew the

answers to every question.
I knew. Now, this morning

I must remember. The head
lines tell of savagery,

slaughter, sorrow; today
I turn away; don't read.

We are the lover.
We are the loved.

The news of children
beaten, raped, missing

    (And what of their first
love, their innocence, Venus?)

We are the lover.
We are the loved.

Those in the womb.
Those in the fire of

transformation. Those who
dream under Venus, only to

wake under the Morning Star,
trying to remember the answer.

We are the lover.
We are the loved.

Every color we are.
Every tongue we are.

Silent and singing with love,
hate, fear, joy; but remember,

please remember, we are all
innocent, tired children dreaming:

we cry, we remember
our very first love, always

in the delicate, fragile
light of the Morning Star.

We are the lover.
We are the loved.

(The Rainbow Heart)
Someone, a total stranger,
in fact, a beautiful young

man with earrings in both
ears, asked me what I

wanted—he pointed to the
row of stickers behind

him as I paid for
food—I looked up at

him and said, "What?"
"Which one do you want?"

There were bears, cats,
stars, moons, suns—

I stared as he waited—
"I'll take the rainbow

heart." I placed the tiny
gift over my own stubborn,

muscled, human heart and
I thanked him.

I am the lover.
I am the loved.

CALIFORNIA POPPY

Most of the kids in my fifth-grade
class in the Mission, San Francisco,
were brown, black, some white,
most poor, some with real

families, some money—and the
White Lady Teacher said:
"The California poppy is the state
flower, you must *never* pick

it, you must *never* pick
it, you must *never* pick
it, that's the law."
And I remember walking home that

day from the White Lady Teacher's
class, down the alley where kids
met to fight, and I fought there
twice with boys, and both times

I made them bleed and cry, so
I won; and there they were.
The flowers I should *never* pick,
the flowers I should *never* pick,

the flowers I should *never* pick,
that's the law. And I remember her
saying one time to some girls, "You'll
have babies by the time you're 16,

girls like you," and I knew
she was talking to me as I flushed
hot with shame and anger, anger and
shame. So, I picked one California poppy,

stuffed it in my pocket till it died.
And later, I picked 2, 3, 4, 5
and ate them too, and then I glared
and smiled at the White Lady Teacher

as the California poppy bloomed
inside me, fueled by
the heat of my heart.
Now, 42 years later, I close

my eyes and I see California extending
the coast to the southern tip of Chile, to
the northern tip of Nome. I close
my eyes and see north to south, south

to north, as birds fly, as whales
swim pregnant with their young,
butterflies dreaming, dripping from coastal
trees—porpoises, otters, seals, sharks, eagles,

hawks, bears, mountain lions, jaguars,
wolves, humans—north to south, south
to north for centuries. I close my eyes
and see my California poppy on
fire.

*   *   *

I was born in California, beautiful,
holy, so sacred California.
I was poor in California, and hungry
in California. I have stolen food as

a child in California.
I stole baby clothes when
I was pregnant at 15 in California.
I was punished for speaking Spanish

in school when I was 6 and learned
to speak English in California, in California.
All my children—born when I was 15, 17,
21, 36—were born in sacred California.

My 2 grandchildren were born in
holy, so sacred California.

I've been on welfare in California.
I've been married in California.

I've been unmarried in California.
I've been beaten in California.
I've been raped in California.
I've been healed in California, yes,

in this beautiful, holy, oh so sacred
California. I learned to write in English,
hearing my grandmother's voice, voices of my
ancestors, in sacred California.

I close my eyes and I see
California extending the coast to the
southern tip of Chile, to the
northern tip of Nome.

I close my eyes and I see
north to south, south to north,
as birds fly, as whales swim
pregnant with their young,

butterflies dreaming, dripping from
coastal trees—porpoises, otters, seals,
sharks, eagles, hawks, bears, mountain
lions, jaguars, wolves, humans—

north to south, south to north,
for centuries. I close
my eyes and see
my California poppy on

fire. Blooming, dying,
blooming; fueled by—
fueled by the heat—
fueled by the heat of—

fueled by the heat of my—
fueled by the heat

of my borderless
heart.

*(With the shadow of California Proposition 187 in
mind, which is hostile to the newcomer. And to all those
suffering and dying because of human-made borders
everywhere on our planet, especially the children who,
naturally and rightfully, feel at home everywhere on
Earth until they're taught not to.)*

ONE LAST LONG HOWL

GREEN ENCHILADAS FOR BREAKFAST

As the visiting writer, I'm
put in the Butterfly Room;
butterflies, real ones (now
dead), framed in gold; paintings

of butterflies framed in gold;
butterflies woven into the antique
couch, on the bedspread, paper
ones clipped to the chandelier;

and outside, lemon-yellow butterflies,
lime-green butterflies, orange and
white butterflies filter the sun, gliding,
gliding with perfect ease. I sit transfixed

in the Texas sun, so close to Mexico
they fly both flags (USA/MEXICO)
side by side. The loud, braying
laughter of Mexican women makes me

smile, suddenly, and turn to see
the wild, confident hussy; she's young,
she's old, a wicked shine in her eyes:
"Yes, they tried to break my spirit too,

I've seen better and I've seen worse;
do you like your butterflies; do you like
the Butterfly Room; there, spread your
wet wings, it's time for your new life,

the next one; you will laugh so loudly
people will turn and mutter; your voice
will be full of satisfaction, and your tears
normal as rain; now, bless this room,

this Butterfly Room, where women
have come forever to be made
new; you were not born to be a mother,
you were not born to be a wife or

simply a lover; you were not born to
please, heal, destroy, or even to
create. You were born to enter the
Butterfly Room and emerge when you're

damn well ready. These are your wings.
These are your colors. This is
your very own life. This is
the sun and air. It is time.

It is time to fly.
Flags mean nothing to you.
You dream pleasure, pain,
as you glide with perfect

ease (children, sex, hunger,
thirst, blood, sperm, terror,
wonder) into your next life.
Forget and remember. Remember

and forget. This is
the place of remembering
and forgetting. It's (almost)
better than sex.

It may be better than
laughter. The only thing worse
is to allow your spirit to be stolen,
to be hung in a golden frame."

Green enchiladas for breakfast.
I sit in the Texas sun, facing
a slow-moving river.
I remember to forget.

I forget to remember.
I remember love in my body,
in my butterfly body, and
I forget to die, again.

San Antonio, Texas
Día de los Muertos,
Day of the Dead, 1996

THE REAL SACRED GAME

I feed stray cats
every morning just as
Venus sets, and I
don't love you anymore.

I wake up, make my coffee,
fix my hair, watch the
sun, her shadow, and I
don't love you anymore.

I go shopping for fresh
mushrooms, red onions,
ripe avocados, and I
don't love you anymore.

I buy sunflowers, white
and purple orchids, tiny
Christmas trees, and I
don't love you anymore.

I watch my son go surfing
under the Full Moon in winter,
and we laugh, and I
don't love you anymore.

I watched you leave and break
his heart, his trusting, young
man's heart, and I don't, I
don't love you anymore.

I read the badly written poem
you wrote to some unsuspecting
woman—it makes me laugh—I
don't love you anymore.

I see your pot belly,
your balding head, the fat
man I used to love, and I
don't love you anymore.

I see a middle-aged man
with hemorrhoids, who drives
a 2nd-hand Porsche, and I really
don't love you anymore.

I hear the EGO, the enormous
cruelty in your voice—
you bore me, in short, I
don't love you anymore.

Your lack of presence in
my world renders every
thing fresh—pain and joy—I
don't love you anymore.

Men friends can call me
now, and I can think of men who
I've loved—the dead, the living—I
don't love you anymore.

Your stupid jealousies, never
ending—I'd feel sorry for
you, then angry—I sure
don't love you anymore.

             *   *   *

But I *did* treasure our "sacred
bond"—I chose you over wealth,
beauty, the compliments of
sweet, young men—I chose

you for the soul you kept
under lock and key—I found
the key, you changed the lock,
our game, our sacred

game, played too often,
grew predictable—how long
could I wait for you to
detach from Wild Kingdom

at 1 am, or to understand
that a trip to the beach
would be sandy, to watch
the golden moon rise you must

be patient, to scatter a loved
one's ashes you must weep,
to love a nearly grown son
you must watch his body for

injuries, his stomach for
hunger, his eyes for
sadness, and be on call in
case his friends are drinking, driving—

to be the one who sets
limits, curfews, chores—
to be the one who will set
him free to Life—

to be the one he can be angry
at, and be the one who won't
leave—
to be the one who feels

his daily pain, his love
for you, his daily
father, what you took.
Do you realize what you took?

Do you realize what you've
lost? I doubt it.
You think you're *free*,
that Death has lost

your old address, that
you've escaped the round
of human cycles, human
love—pain and joy.

But I must tell you,
your soul and Death are
old friends, old lovers
(the real Sacred Game)—

they live in the same sacred
house—one is the lock,
one is the key—*you are*
their sacred bond.

This is your blessing.
This is your curse.
Under lock and key.
Your freedom. To love.

This takes real courage.
The lock. The key.
Daily chores. The Soul.
And Death. In love.

*   *   *

Hungry cats. Venus rising.
Sliced mushrooms. Flowers in water.
My son surfing under the
Full Moon. I see his

soul, his Death, in
fearless harmony, his
willingness to love a
balding, middle-aged fat

man with hemorrhoids who
drives a 2nd-hand Porsche,
who took his father with
him, who has no interest in

his daily victories, his daily
defeats, who doesn't under
stand the beauty of
a son who surfs by

moonlight in the frigid
winter sea (the lock,
the key). And I just
don't love you anymore.

December, Full Moon, 1997

CHANCE AND DESTINY

What makes me happy
this morning? This bird
of paradise I picked
by the mailbox—I put

it in the bathroom
in water; this morning
a slim, white petal
joined the brilliant

orange ones. This slim,
white petal makes me
happy—a small pine
tree on the kitchen table

with gold stars, gold tassels,
a blue/gold moon ornament
at its tip and tiny golden
spheres dangling from its tiny

branches makes me happy.
The wind and rain from
the sea make me happy,
and the sun that appears

for a moment, creating
rainbows somewhere;
some one watches, the
heart fills with joy,

and though sorrow and all
reasons to grieve continue,
they see the rainbow,
the appearance of the sun,

the scattered leaves of winter,
the wind and rain that whales
love as they journey south.
I am happy because there's

music, poetry, stories to be
read and told, food to be
prepared and eaten, dishes
to be washed, people to be

loved from a great distance,
from so close, and those
I've loved and have set free
in the name of Love,

in the wisdom of beginnings,
and the wisdom of endings—
in the wisdom of the spiral.
(The joy of one slim, white petal.)

   *   *   *

I am happy because
I have seen the
bird of paradise
blooming.

I am happy because
I have seen a lake full
of summer lotus
blooming.

I am happy because
I have tangerines, apples,
bananas and a pumpkin on
my table.

I am happy because
I was born 53 years
ago, and that I'm here,
now.

I am happy for where
I've been and I am happy
for where I'm going
to.

I am happy because
the world is so beautiful
and mysterious, and I am
welcome.

*   *   *

I am like the slim, white
petal, blooming in the bird
of paradise, by chance.
And destiny.

December 1997, Santa Cruz
To my eldest son (at thirty-five), Ed

> "The first innocence is given,
> the second is chosen."
> —Wise person, anon.

November 30, 1997

DEAR WORLD,

Who are the guilty?
Who are the murderers?
Who are the insane?
Who are the evil?
Who are the unloved?
Who are the rapists?
Who are the unguilty?
Who are the innocent?

While certain dictators dream of
invisible viruses floating through
the air, killing their enemies, killing
everyone but themselves, killing

the guilty and the innocent, equally—
while dreaming of weaponry that will
finally give them safety and peace,
populated by a planet of conquered YES.

While the young skinheads in Denver hate
a man from West Africa so much, they
kill him because his skin is the color of
pure dreams and the sun's light loved him.

While my 16-year-old son shaves his head
for freedom to run and surf, and he hates
the idea of hitting or being hit—he is gentler
than I, born on Martin Luther King's birthday.

While China's leaders keep its dissident heroes in prison
for decades, and Tibet under its terrible rule,
then punish their heroes by exiling
them from their land and people—

167

and while I love ancient Chinese poetry,
wisdom, the art of stillness, essence,
beauty—I believe the Chinese *people*
simply want to live, love, laugh, weep, live.

And while there are mad men who send
bombs through the mail from their tiny
cabins in the wild, there's a harmless
mad man in my neighborhood who wanders

barefoot in a T-shirt, stringy hair—the windows
of his tiny cabin (on a busy street) are streaked
with soap and eggs, and he harms no one
but himself (like a saint).

While a 19-year-old woman was picked up in
Mexico by the police because she wanted her
people to have food, housing, education, justice—
while I shopped at Lucky's, did my laundry,

sent my words for publication,
she was tortured and raped.
All the young women, all the young men,
all the families, their children, in Mexico, Central

and South America, who fight (some are killed)
for the privilege of living, while
I balance my diet and exercise,
write letters for Amnesty International, this poem.

While a 22-year-old student named Lara,
in Venezuela, is held in jail because
she speaks out for simple freedom—
while her family has been told by witnesses

she was beaten and dragged away—
they haven't seen her as I write this
poem, and nothing can be done in this
place where torture and rape is as common

as sunlight, moonlight, starlight, the songs
of birds, the flight of rainbow butterflies,
the child's first step, the child's first
smile, the child's first laughter, first

delight, and cries of hunger, discomfort,
quickly stilled by the rounded, full breast,
warm arms, soothing heart beat we all
remember from the innocence of the

womb.
While a 14-year-old boy in Kentucky kills
other children, then says, "Kill me now"—
he killed his friends, while his heart

beat drove him on to steal the gun,
bring it to school, fire it without knowing
why (he had to); unable to choose
his innocence, he killed the innocence

of others, and stilled their hearts to
silence. While we all (murderers, torturers,
rapists and their victims) remember, if we
can *stand the silence,* if we

can stand in the silence, if we
can understand the silence—
the heart beat of the Universe
all around, all around

us. While the Universe waits
for us to listen, we are
forgiven and loved,
loved and forgiven.

While men and women give their
lives for others, and those who simply
heal the body and the soul—
while others save the from

extinction, and others teach cranes
how to migrate, and others take to the
sea, climb buildings like mountains,
unfurl their banners, unfurl their spirits,

to save our planet,
to save us all.
While the Universe waits
for us to listen, we are

loved and forgiven,
forgiven and loved.
While a 14-year-old girl
named Anne Frank witnessed

cruelties I'll never know, daily, nightly,
in a German concentration camp (starvation,
beatings, death in inhuman numbers)—cruelties
as common as hot chocolate, warm muffins

from the oven, a patch of luminous
sky, clouds in the shape of racing horses,
someone's face you remember, you loved,
and I wonder if she had the comfort of clouds

in that place of no silence,
the screaming dead, yes, I wonder.
On July 15, 1944 (3 months before
I was born, still in the womb, listening),

this 14-year-old girl wrote:
". . . in spite of everything I still believe
people are good at heart." At heart.
In the heart. In the womb.

She gave me innocence.
She died when I was 5 months old, but not
her innocence. (She gives us innocence.)
She chose

to forgive and love,
to love and forgive,
while the Universe waits—
stand in the silence—

the heart beat of the Universe
all around,
all around.
Listen.

(To the work of Amnesty International and Greenpeace,
their inexhaustible innocence, inspiration—
their belief in the human heart.
And to my youngest son, Jules.)

Errata

P. 169, stanza 8, line 4:
read "while others
save the wolf from"